that did not happen. "So I know why you are so mad, Jason. You can't read, can you?"

I promised Jason that his teacher and I knew how to teach him to read and that we would teach him this year. I explained that I understood if he did not believe me, but assured him that within a month he would realize that he was learning to read.

Jason began to cry and, between sobs, asked me if I would eat lunch with him. When I looked back in the records, I noted that one of Jason's punishments for not completing his work correctly was to be isolated at lunch. During lunch, Jason asked me if I was going to call his mother. I worried that Jason would be concerned that I would tell his mother that he could not read. So I explained that I would give him my number and he could have his mother call me if he wanted her to talk with me. To my surprise, Jason wanted my number and told me his mother would want to call me, that she had been hoping someone would teach him to read.

Why didn't Jason learn to read with the other five-year-olds? Was it one of the commonly offered explanations — because he wasn't smart enough or because his family did not support the school or because he didn't work hard enough or because he didn't care? None of those explanations fit his personality or his home life or his reactions to his reading disability.

Jason was thin and small for his age. His face was pale, his lips were blue, and he would often stop to catch his breath. Talking with Jason's mother, I learned that Jason had open heart surgery during his first year of kindergarten. After surgery, he was absent for many days and on large dosages of medication when he returned to school. Most likely, that is the reason Jason did not learn to read with the other five-year-olds. Consequently, he became confused about print and, from that point on, traditional reading instruction baffled him.

Unfortunately, Jason's problem went undiagnosed. With early detection of his confusion about print and the necessary action of a prescribed learning program, Jason would never have suffered from the disability of illiteracy. Jason became a reader during his fifth year of school, his behavior at school improved, and he continues to make progress in his reading abilities. It is unlikely Jason ever will be able to completely heal his wounds of being a non-reader in a world of words for so long.

When once children like Jason might have been doomed to become statistics, they no longer need to face futures of hardship and unfulfilled promise. These children are part of an identifiable group of students who are at risk of reading failure. Through routine diagnostic procedures and trained teacher observation, they can be identified at the beginning of their kindergarten year. As emergent, at-risk readers, they then become participants in a reading program designed especially for them.

Early Detection Necessary Action has evolved over many years and is based on my own experiences, the experiences of other educators, and a thorough review of the literature used in reading instruction. My observation is that teachers are not trained to teach reading to students who need alternative methods of instruction. Colleges and universities do not provide this valuable information to elementary education majors. Only educators who receive advanced degrees in the area of reading learn how to teach these students. Elementary teachers must develop the expertise to teach all students in the normal classroom setting. E.D.N.A. provides teachers with this knowledge and opens the doors to a lifetime of learning for students who otherwise might be lost forever.

Early detection is an essential ingredient in eliminating the stigma of being set apart as a "non-reader." Taking the necessary action prevents reinforcing the ineffective strategies employed by the at-risk student in order to cope as a non-reader. With E.D.N.A., you will learn how to take that action.

- You will learn how to identify at-risk, emergent readers and how to teach them.
- You will be able to evaluate exactly what your at-risk students know.
- You will know precisely what those students need to know next.
- You will be provided the appropriate materials needed to teach these students.
- You will thoroughly understand the effective, sequential steps to carry out the program.
- You will be taught the skills to effectively monitor the student's progress and you will understand how to adjust the instruction accordingly.
- You will know how to give students the opportunity to practice doing what good readers do.
- You will enable your at-risk students to progress from learning to read to reading to learn.

Instruction is the most important function of an educator, and student achievement is the ultimate goal. All students can learn and are of equal worth. When a student does not learn, it is the fault of the program, not the fault of the student. Therefore, the program must change. The educational program should allow the student to earn justified praise and experience success.

As educators, it is our responsibility to provide strategies and methods of instruction to teach students who are at various instructional levels and who have individual learning styles. All students must view the school as their own and be invited and welcomed into the learning experience.

We, the educational community, hold the future of all students in our hands. Failure is not an option. I invite you to share in my vision, my dream, and my prayer that all children who are like Jason will receive the help they need when they need it and that all children who are like my talented friend will have the help they need to learn to read when they are six, not twenty-six.

For purposes of clarity in this book, I refer to teachers using the pronoun *she* and to students with the pronoun *he*. This is simply an editorial decision in order to avoid confusion within the text of the book.

Failure Is Not An Option

Chapter One

The At-Risk Student

By the time Mark enters first grade, he has been labeled a "slow learner." His performance throughout the first grade year does little to dispel the validity of this classification, and by the end of the year, his teacher feels she has no choice. Mark is retained.

Jesse is a student whose hyperactivity is exacerbated by constant, ongoing ear infections. About the time the cycle of medication is complete for one infection, another sets in.

Sitting next to Jesse near the window is Laura. She is every teacher's delight. Her parents, both college educated, are committed to Laura's success as a student, and, indeed, all of the signs point to the promise of a good student. Laura is attentive and studious. She is verbally expressive and has an impressive vocabulary, though often her verb tenses are incorrect. She delights in standing before her classmates to retell a story from a book.

At the back of the room, in the row closest to the door, sits Maggie. Unlike Laura, Maggie would never dream of standing at the front of the classroom to tell about anything, much less the story from a book. When Maggie is forced by the teacher to participate in class, she whispers a tentative response punctuated by a question mark made by the inflection of her voice and the troubled expression on her face.

The fluorescent lights in the classroom seem to bother Jerome. They cast a glare on his paper. Letters are distorted and words appear blurred. Because it is uncomfortable for him to physically focus on his work, he simply does not look at it.

During the first week of school, the teacher is talking with her students about a book they are going to read. It is about a shrimp boat, and she relates it to experiences they may have had during the summer vacation. Jesse's summer cold is getting worse. He can breathe only through his mouth because of the congestion. His ears are beginning to close up and throb and he is running a low-grade fever.

Laura struggles to hear her teacher's explanation of the book. It is hard to hear with Jesse's labored breathing on one side of her and the roar of the air conditioner on the other. She is intrigued by the pictures, though, and pays close attention to the teacher.

Maggie sits quietly, her head bowed thoughtfully over the book on her desk. She misunderstands parts of the story and is confused by some of the letters. They often look alike to her.

Jerome, on the other hand, is not interested at all. Focusing on the book makes his head feel funny, and the words and pictures all look weird. Why pay attention when it hurts and is so strange anyway?

And then there is Grady. Grady is from a large family whose Mother works several jobs to make ends meet. She is rarely at home, and Grady and his siblings are in the care of an older sister, a sixteen-year-old high school dropout. The only books Grady has seen are at school, and he does not seem to have an interest in any of them. No one has ever sat down with Grady and read to him. When the teacher tells the class they are going to talk about the shrimp boat, Grady has no idea it could be anything other than a restaurant near his house. It is called "The Shrimp Boat."

There are six students in this first-grade class who are at risk of never learning how to read.

How would you know? To the untrained eye, their problems do not seem so unusual or noticeable or even unique. After all, many students are retained each year. For that matter, what classroom doesn't have its share of hyper children, or those who seem to suffer from constant ear or sinus infections? Who would guess that an enthusiastic student, eager to please, would have anything to hide? Why would the teacher be overly concerned about the quiet child, when it is all she can do to corral the impulsive one? And, admit it. Isn't it just a little humorous, even endearing, that some children might think a shrimp boat is the name of a restaurant and nothing more?

Who are the six students in this first-grade class who are at risk of never learning how to read?
- One has been retained.
- Another has auditory interference due to chronic ear infections.
- Yet another has central auditory processing difficulties.
- The fourth one is shy.
- One has uncorrected vision problems.

- The sixth one has a severely limited background of experience.

There is no more critical step in the process of teaching reading than in diagnosing the at-risk student. Before an effective learning plan can be implemented, before reading material can be chosen, before bad habits take root, before practice makes permanent, the problem must be identified.

Who Is At Risk?

Retention

At the top of the at-risk list are those students who have been retained.

Why is a student a candidate for retention? Is he not being taught? Is he unable to learn? Those of us who are teachers would answer unequivocally that this student is most certainly being taught, just as the other students in the classroom are being taught, and he is, in fact, able to learn, for there are other slow learners who are able to move forward.

A student is a candidate for retention because he is not being taught the appropriate material. It is not because the teacher is not teaching, because she is. It is not because the student does not want to learn, because he does. It is because the program he is being taught is not suitable for him.

Educators know that the act of retaining is often devastating to a student. It is not nearly as devastating, though, as another year spent teaching this student the same material that so greatly confused him the first time. By the end of his second year in the same grade, his confusion has grown insurmountably. Rather than curing the problems which led to his retention, we have added to them.

If the program is not working, change it. If a student is not learning, teach him differently. Do not ever retain a student and teach him using the same material. It did not work the first time. It will not ever work for this child.

There is no greater lesson to be learned than the one taught to both educators and parents by a retained student. It is easy to learn, simple and straight-forward, and it makes perfect sense: If a student must be retained, he must be taught differently. The first way did not work. Practice does not make perfect. Practice makes permanent.

Too often, retention guarantees the student will be taught using the same methods and materials. Too often, retention is a plan for remediation. Too often, retention becomes a learning activity. Too often, retention provides an opportunity to practice mistakes.

The truth is that retention has few, if any, redeeming characteristics. If retention is used as a plan for making the student an effective reader, it will have everlasting and devastating effects. Retention only reinforces bad habits and behavior. Retention dramatically increases the chances that the student will eventually drop out of school. Some studies show dropout rates as high as 60% to 90% for children who have been retained.

Before a student is considered a candidate for retention, change the learning program for him, and if you are teaching a student who has been retained, do not teach him using the same material. Do not give him an opportunity to practice what does not work.

The process of evaluating a student for retention should include these two questions: Why didn't this student learn when the other children learned? Will another year do it?

Learning to read is enough of a challenge for six- and seven-year-old students. Do not make retention another hurdle they must jump. Be careful about retention. It is rarely the answer.

Mark is lucky this year. His new teacher is well aware of the fact that this is Mark's second try at first grade. She also knows it will do neither of them any good to repeat the mistakes of the previous year. She will remember all the things that did not work last year, and she will concentrate on the things which do work. A new, prescribed method of learning will be taught to Mark.

The administration has provided Mark's teacher with the appropriate training, and she now has the knowledge and experience to effectively teach Mark. Additionally, she has been provided the proper books and materials Mark needs, both at his present level and at his grade placement. The administration has organized the students within the school in such a way that Mark's teacher has time to teach Mark as well as the other students in her classroom who are on and above their grade placement.

Because of the teacher's knowledge and the administration's support, Mark will learn to read this year.

Auditory Interference

Students who have auditory interference are also at-risk of reading failure. Included in this category are students who have fluid behind the ears, chronic ear infections, hearing loss, and central auditory processing difficulties. Both Jesse and Laura are examples of students with this at-risk factor, though their individual problems differ.

Chronic Ear Infections

Jesse suffers from chronic ear infections and fluid behind his ears. He simply cannot hear, and because of this condition, he passes from one day to another without the ability to distinguish sounds.

A typical week for Jesse goes like this:
On Monday when his teacher is teaching the letter *d* using *d*og, *d*oll and *d*ress as examples, Jesse hears the words, but is distracted by an annoying runny nose, a thumping in his ears and a bit of a headache. On Tuesday, Jesse's congestion is worse, his sinuses are clogged, and the infection has found a nesting ground deep in his ear canals. When his teacher reviews *d*og, *d*oll, and *d*ress, the only sound Jesse is able to hear is the *s* at the end of the word *dress*. When his teacher says, "*dress*," and points to the *d*, Jesse only hears the *s*.

On Wednesday, Jesse's mother wisely takes him to the doctor who diagnoses a sinus and ear infection and prescribes medicine. Because of his absence, Wednesday's lessons are lost to Jesse, but on Thursday he is back in the classroom. The antibiotic he is taking for the infection makes his stomach hurt and the antihistamine intended to relieve the congestion makes him either hyper or drowsy, depending on the dosage. It is no wonder Jesse has little concentration for Thursday's lesson, and the little he does have just reinforces his belief that the *d* sounds like the *s*. On the last day of the school week, Jesse's condition is improving. His congestion has loosened, and he is hearing somewhat better.

And just what is Jesse hearing? He is hearing the *s* every time he sees the *d*. In Jesse's mind, the *s* sound is forever linked up with the *d*. He is unable to associate the right sound with the right symbol. His confusion will have debilitating consequences.

Central Auditory Processing Difficulties

Laura also has difficulty hearing the teacher. She hears Jesse sniffing and coughing. She hears the noises of the outside world just beyond the window where she sits. She hears the air conditioner turning on and off during the warm days of autumn and spring, and she hears the heater grinding through the cold days of winter. She is disturbed by the annoying hum of the overhead projector. Laura's world is filled with constant noise — loud, thundering, disruptive noise. Laura has a freight train running through her ears that no one else can hear.

Laura's auditory interference is defined as "the inability to understand spoken language in a meaningful way even though there is no hearing loss." In other words, Laura suffers from Central Auditory Processing Difficulties. So severe is Laura's auditory interference that she is unable to separate background noise from the sound of her teacher's voice.

While Laura is attentive to her teacher, she is able to process little of what her teacher says. Noises which fade into the background for the rest of us prevent Laura from hearing anything other than bits and pieces of her teacher's instruction. If those instructions are complex, given rapidly, or are lengthy, Laura becomes even more confused.

A suspicious teacher might wonder why Laura's vocabulary is broad, but her verb tenses are wrong. A curious teacher might question why Laura always chooses to tell a story to the class, rather than read it to the class. An astute teacher will acknowledge both of those mysteries and will proceed to discover why they are happening. This teacher will know that Laura's family is highly educated and, while that might account for the fact that Laura uses impressive words, it does not explain why she is unable to discriminate between proper and improper verb tenses. This teacher will learn that Laura's best friend reads the books to Laura who then is able to present herself before the class to retell the story. Most importantly, this teacher will discover that Laura is hindered by central auditory processing difficulties, a problem for which she is able to receive help.

In the first week of school, Laura and Jesse's teacher will administer a Phonemic Awareness Test and an Oral Language Survey to all of her students. The students who score less than eighty percent are the students with possible auditory interference. The teacher will then complete a checklist which profiles the Observable Clues To Classroom Auditory Problems. She will also conduct an Auditory Memory Test and an Auditory Discrimination Test. Students who score below eighty percent will have difficulty with auditory discrimination.

Before any measurable instructional time goes by, this teacher will learn that Jesse has a history of chronic ear infections and that, when he is not well, he is also not hearing. She will understand that, when Jesse *is* well, he is confused because of misconceptions his temporary hearing loss, due to the infection, has caused.

She will learn that Laura, whose problems are not as physically obvious, needs to be evaluated by an audiologist and speech-language pathologist, and, in the meantime, she will move Laura away from the window and will place her desk closer to the front of the room. In addition, the teacher will discover if any of her students suffer permanent hearing losses, or, at the very least, alert her to the fact that this might be true for some students.

Without these diagnostic tools, Jesse would just be another one of those unfortunate students who never seems to escape an infection, and Laura would continue trying desperately to be a good student for her unsuspecting teacher. Both would proceed from one moment to the next with mounting confusion.

Like Mark, Laura and Jesse are going to have a productive year in school. They are on the right track, headed toward a destination of reading fluency, and they have their teacher to thank.

Visual Interference

Visual Interference is the third at-risk factor. Students with uncorrected vision problems, poor visual memory, those who have difficulty focusing, and have problems distinguishing figures from background or distinguishing similar letter shapes from each other, those who are impulsive and hyper, and children who are shy, all fall into this category. Some children who suffer from visual interference are actually lucky, for their problems can be corrected.

Think about Jerome, who avoids looking at print because of the glare on the paper and the distorted shapes of the words. To try to focus on a page of words makes Jerome's head hurt. To make matters worse, his eyes do not seem to work together. One sees one thing, the other another. His confusion is overwhelming. Consequently, Jerome has no visual memory. He might look at an a or a d, but he cannot remember them. An F, T, L, and K all look alike to him. When he does look at a page of print, he either sees the white spaces and disregards the letters, or he sees nothing but letters which to him look like blobs of black.

Jerome's teacher has absolutely no way of knowing what Jerome's eyes are seeing, and without the proper diagnostic measures, Jerome could go for years without having his vision problems corrected. By then, his reading confusion will be overwhelming and will require an enormous effort to correct.

In the first week of school, though, when Jerome's teacher is acquainting herself with Mark who is in first grade for the second time, and she is preparing to administer the auditory tests which will identify Jesse and Laura's problems, she also has set aside time to evaluate the vision of her new students. She knows not to rely solely on the Snellen Chart. It measures vision only at a distance, not up close where books are held for reading. Her checklist of Observable Clues To Classroom Vision Problems, the Visual Discrimination Test, and the Visual Memory Test help identify early on the problems of several of her students.

Jerome's teacher learns enough about Jerome's eyesight to advise his parents to have him evaluated by an ophthalmologist or optician. When the report is concluded, Jerome has been diagnosed with a slight astigmatism. Instead of being shaped symmetrically, somewhat like a basketball, the corneas of Jerome's eyes are shaped more like a football, preventing light rays from converging in a single focal point to create a crisp visual image. It is understandable that the glare on the paper from the fluorescent lights is bothersome to Jerome.

Jerome is also diagnosed with eye-teaming difficulties which prevent him from focusing on one word at a time. His eyes simply do not work as a team. Being able to focus on print, to use a finger to point to each word and work across a line of print from left to right is a physical skill.

The children who have difficulty with this skill more often than not have eyes which simply do not work together. Successful eye teaming is critical in learning how to read. It is a skill often taken for granted, but imagine for a moment how difficult it would be to read this line of print if your eyes were working in opposition to each other. Jerome's new glasses, which correct his astigmatism, also help his eye-teaming problems.

Of further benefit is his teacher's assistance in helping Jerome learn to follow a line of words from left to right using his finger to point to each word, one at a time. Students with eye-teaming difficulties often will attempt to read from right to left, or top to bottom, or bottom to top, reading stacks of words, rather than strings of sentences. Some students read in a snaking pattern; that is, they follow words from the left side of the page to within a few words near the end of the line, then drop their eyes to the same point on the next line, reading from right to left. The confusion these students experience is understandable. How must the story sound to them? What meaning can they possibly receive from the words?

The inability to focus on print and have the eyes work as one, moving together across a line of print is called eye teaming. Without it, a student is lost.

Jerome is fortunate to have his vision problems identified and corrected, but prior to the diagnosis, he was well on his way to establishing some major reading problems. His flight from print, caused by the physical discomfort he felt when he looked at a page of words, was presenting another problem for Jerome. Poor visual memory affects those students who simply cannot remember what letters look like. They can look at a letter but cannot remember it from one time to the next. Some letters look identical. They simply see no differences in the shapes of certain letters. They possess no memory of the print they have seen and consequently cannot discriminate between letters, especially those which look so much alike: *F* and *T*; *f* and *t*; *d* and *b*; *M* and *N*; *m* and *n*, for instance. Think of the similarity of so many letters in the alphabet. For a student with poor visual memory, the list is endless, and the confusion is staggering.

Children who look at a page of print and see the white spaces surrounding the letters have figure-ground difficulties. This way of looking at a page of print indicates that these students cannot discriminate between the words and the page on which they are printed, that one is dominate over the other, and that neither relates to the other. When a student has figure-ground difficulties, he sees the background, not the print.

Children with visual-configuration problems see only the print. Rather than identifying letters and words, however, this student sees the blackness of the print. His identification of the letter *d*, for instance, is not a figure shaped with a stick and a ball. The student with visual-configuration problems sees a blob of black.

Attention Disorder

Hyper children also fit into the Visual Interference at-risk category. They simply cannot attend to print. These students, impulsive in nature, are often the same children who are diagnosed as having attention deficit disorders. The A.D.D. student is not in control of his inattentiveness, but because of his behavior, he misses out completely on the page of print in front of him. Slight variances in letters and words go unnoticed, and the big picture is a blur. While this child is missing out on valuable lessons, the unfortunate thing is that his behavior is preventing others from learning, also, especially those children who are already at risk and have their own difficulties to conquer.

<u>Shy and Timid</u>
Then there are the children like Maggie who want so desperately to be perfect. Maggie is painfully shy. To speak up, to take a chance, to offer an answer is a risk she just is not willing to take. What if she were to stammer, or guess incorrectly, or give the wrong answer? How silly she would look! If only Maggie could be perfect. There are others in her classroom who are, she thinks. Perfect would be just fine for Maggie, but she isn't, and she knows it. She avoids participating, and because of her quite nature, she is overlooked, left alone, not bothered. When she learns a lesson incorrectly, no one knows. Not even Maggie.

For timid children, looking at print and not understanding it is a risk not worth taking, so they avoid it altogether. Anything new scares them because it presents a situation where mistakes can be made. These children want to please. They do not want anyone to be disappointed in them. They never participate in classroom discussions, would not choose ever to answer a direct question, and when they are drawn outside of their protective shell, they answer tentatively and quietly, hoping at the very most to be right, and at the very least, to not be heard at all.

Maggie will not participate in class. She is afraid to take a chance, and because the prospect of making a mistake haunts her, she has withdrawn without even trying. Maggie is content not being noticed. Who will know her confusion?

Of all the problems presented so far, the least challenging is Jerome's vision problem. The diagnosis is like a breath of fresh air to his teacher. Though she would choose for Jerome to have perfect eyesight, his difficulties can at least be corrected. Children whose eye problems go uncorrected will not have spontaneous recovery because of their misconceptions regarding print. How they see print with undiagnosed and uncorrected vision problems becomes how they will always see it. Correcting even slight vision problems is critical to the success of an emergent reader.

The remaining problems associated with visual interference, as well as the other at-risk factors, create more of a challenge in the classroom. If only a pair of glasses would work for everyone.

While Jerome's vision disorder is the only one of the at-risk factors which can be *corrected*, the last at-risk factor — Limited Background of Experience — can be *fixed*.

Limited Background

Remember Grady? His only exposure to books is at school. His ability to converse is limited because it is not a skill he has needed or practiced. Children who are not exposed to language and books are automatically at a disadvantage. If they do not have the experience of having heard words, in expanding their basic vocabulary, they are unable to match words with what would make sense in the meaning of the story. When children have not heard good, fluent, proper, standard English, they are disabled in a way which makes learning difficult.

The good news is that these children can be given the experience and background. When the teacher recognizes that these children have not had experiences to aid them as they learn, she simply tells them everything they need to know. A lot of work? Yes, indeed, but a limited background of experience is the easiest at-risk factor to fix, and fix it, we must.

Any single, given classroom might have as many as two thirds of the students who exhibit a limited background of experience. After administering the Oral Language Survey, the teacher is able to identify those children who have limited language skills, limited sentence structure, limited vocabulary, limited experiences, and poor auditory discrimination of sounds. While a student's failure to score eighty percent on the Oral Language Survey could indicate a poor literacy background, the same student will score above eighty percent on the Auditory Memory and Auditory Discrimination Tests. With the knowledge provided her by the results of these tests, the teacher's plan of attack is to give these children what they need to know in order to move forward.

Summary

In identifying the students who are at-risk of reading failure, never forget that all students can learn to read. Never forget that some students need to be taught using alternative methods. These are the at-risk children. Children who do not understand print need to be taught about print. Confusion begins at an early age. Children tend to do what they think is right, and for some, this might mean reading from right to left, or thinking that a single letter is a whole word.

Coming to school and not learning affects self-esteem and motivation. A child knows when he is not making progress. Make the reading experience successful for him so he will want to continue reading.

Approach reading as business time. Teach at a table, not on the floor. Make your students attend both physically and mentally. Do not allow them to involve you in their flight from print. Do not allow them to change the subject or look for ways to be sent from the reading group. Never, ever send a child away from a reading group. This is exactly what he wants.

Reading is hard work.

You now know how to identify students who are at risk of never learning how to read. There are six students in this classroom who have been identified and evaluated. An effective reading program is in place for them. It is one which has the instructional material at the student's instructional level and one which regularly monitors the students, telling the teacher what they know and do not know, the strategies they use when they come to a word they do not know, and what they need to know next. The teacher always remembers the importance of assessment. Just because she has taught the material does not mean her students have learned it. She knows to measure the student's ability now against where he was before, and she never measures his performance against that of another student.

This teacher will not soon forget the lessons learned from Mark. She will not use the same material or program he was taught last year. It did not work then, and it will not work now. She has also learned to recognize those students who are not learning along with the rest of the class, and she will not wait until the end of the year to decide that the only choice is retention. Retention is never a choice. Changing the program is.

This teacher knows that Jesse hears just bits and pieces of the material she teaches. She knows he often feels bad. She recognizes Jesse's auditory limitations and has adjusted her teaching accordingly. She speaks distinctly and slowly without exaggerating, and often repeats what she has said. She knows if she points to an *r* and says, "*red*," that Jesse might only hear the *da* sound at the end of the word. She makes sure Jesse sees her lips and that he hears the sound of the letter to which she is pointing. Those are the facts of Jesse's life, and knowing this, his teacher is an enormous help in eliminating and diminishing his confusion.

This teacher is attuned to the ample clues Laura gives of her auditory processing difficulties: looking confused when directions are given; paying close attention but not understanding; using verb tenses incorrectly; and retelling rather than reading a book. She instructs Laura in much the same manner she instructs Jesse, understanding that these children simply do not hear everything they need to hear. She has moved Laura's desk to the front of the class, away from as many distractions as possible.

Jerome proudly sports new glasses. Occasionally, he forgets and leaves them at home. He and his teacher have set aside a special place for Jerome's glasses, a place of honor in her desk. At the end of the school day, Jerome feels privileged to be able to open the drawer of his teacher's desk and place his glasses there to await him the next morning.

Maggie is feeling more secure as her teacher pulls her out of her shell, congratulating her on her successes and seeing her through her mistakes. "Are you supposed to know all the answers?" her teacher asks Maggie, who nods a shy yes. "Of course you aren't. You're only six years old. If you knew all the answers, there wouldn't be any need for you to come to school. And I would be out of a job!" her teacher says. Maggie laughs. She is making progress.

Grady is building his background of experience through the books he is reading and the conversations he is having on a regular basis with his teacher. He loves reading about the shrimp boat, how its nets are lowered from the sides of the boat and, like the wings of a bird, flap down into the water. He knows the nets scoop the shrimp from the ocean and dump them into the boat, and when the boat is back in port, the shrimp are sold to local restaurants, maybe even to "The Shrimp Boat" near his house. Grady does not spend nearly as much time with building blocks, puzzles, or at the sandbox now. They do nothing to build his background of experience. Only reading and conversation do that.

These students participate in a daily reading activity which lasts no less than forty-five minutes. Their teacher never allows the reading group to be interrupted. She zealously guards that time, knowing these students will not make progress if they do not practice. She guides them through the learning activities, telling them everything they need to know to decode the words on the page before them. She constantly points out the strategies good readers use.

She knows the only way these students will learn how to read is to practice doing what good readers do when they come to a word they do not know.

Who Is At Risk?

- Students who have been retained.
- Students who have auditory interference:
    - fluid behind the ears
    - chronic ear infections
    - hearing loss
    - auditory memory
    - auditory sequences
    - auditory discrimination
    - background noise
    - interference

- Students with visual interference:
    - uncorrected vision problems
    - poor visual memory
    - difficulty focusing
    - figure ground
    - eye teaming
    - indiscrimination
    - impulsiveness
    - shy, timid children

- Students with a limited background:
    - limited reading experience
    - limited vocabulary
    - limited life experiences
    - limited oral language exposure

Chapter Two

Effective Reading Practices

A successful reading program is the partnership between knowledge and effective practices, and the only way knowledge can prevent reading failure is to get effective practices into the classroom where the students are. Early Detection Necessary Action is designed in such a way as to make it possible for every teacher to use the most effective reading practices with at-risk students.

Effective practices for at-risk readers must include these criteria:

- Monitor and measure their progress in reading regularly.
- Tell them everything they need to know.
- Provide them with many opportunities to practice reading under the guidance of the teacher.
- Have them practice their reading using real books.
- Avoid wasting time on unnecessary activities.
- Instruct them in practicing the skills used by fluent readers.
- Teach them in a small group.
- Sit with them at a table during their instructional lesson.
- Have them practice word recognition skills using all three modalities.

There must be a program in place to regularly measure and monitor the at-risk student's progress in reading.

Many students come to school with one or more of the at-risk factors: auditory interference, visual interference, emotional interference, and/or deficient backgrounds in literacy experiences. This is why there is such an enormous range of differences in children's literacy abilities when they begin school.

In Early Detection Necessary Action, all students are assessed to determine their developmental level and their reading ability in each of the areas that impact their becoming good readers. These measures of reading readiness levels are not taken to label the student. They are not used to justify why the student cannot learn. They are not used to pinpoint those students who are viewed as candidates for retention.

The assessments are taken to discover what the student knows so a determination can be made as to what he needs to learn next. They are taken to identify which students will need substantially larger amounts of instruction than is normally available. The assessments are also used to pinpoint exactly what instruction will accelerate the student in order for him to make normal progress.

In Early Detection Necessary Action, students are evaluated in the following areas: spoken and written language, phonetic analysis, visual analysis, and structural analysis. An assessment is made based on how each student uses his knowledge on these individual skills during real reading and writing situations.

A student's ability to use the skills tested in isolation is evaluated and monitored using a Modified Miscue Inventory and a Writing Survey. These assessments are continuous and ongoing and provide a systematic way for teachers to determine how well their students have learned what has been taught.

The teacher becomes a diagnostician, continuously identifying and making decisions about each student's misconceptions as well as areas of confusion and weakness. Based on her findings, she adjusts her instruction to teach the student exactly what he needs that day to accelerate his reading abilities. Her instruction must be efficient, intensive and on target. Regular analysis of the student's progress ensures that he is developing a perfect understanding of the reading process.

The at-risk reader must receive a Guided Reading Lesson (Described in Chapter Four) at his instructional level under the direction of his teacher every day. In the Guided Reading Lesson, the teacher tells the student everything he needs to know in his preparation to read. She then encourages, directs, and supports the student while he does the work of reading.

The instructional reading level presents material that a student is unable to read with comprehension and understanding without the teacher's instruction and support. When a student is reading at the instructional level, he is reading material with ninety percent accuracy. In other words, he is missing no more than one word in ten. Instructional level means just that: only after the teacher has told the at-risk reader everything he needs to know is he able to read the material. Her instruction allows the student to decipher any unknown elements of print: the names of the characters, the setting, vocabulary words, and any action in the story.

When a student is unable to read material with comprehension and understanding even after the teacher's instructions, he is at his frustration level. Attempting to work on materials at the frustration level forces the student to practice incorrect, ineffective strategies and guarantees reading failure.

At-risk readers must receive direct, thorough, comprehensive pre-reading activities and vocabulary development before they attempt to read the story on their own. While they are reading, the teacher's job is to help them stay at the task of reading which includes coaching, redirecting, supporting and encouraging.

The teacher must refrain from doing the work for the student. She must not, for example, read the story to the student before he is asked to read on his own. She must not demonstrate and interpret the main idea in the story or list the words and explain how the descriptive words build the picture of the characters in the story. The teacher must not supply the correct word when the student comes to a word he does not know.

The teacher's job during the Guided Reading Lesson is to provide guidance, to make sure the student is doing the work of reading, and to have the student practice the strategies used by good readers. The purpose of the Guided Reading Lesson is to develop the skills the student must have in order to become an independent reader.

Teaching the at-risk reader to read and make progress in reading is not complicated nor is the process a mystery. But it is hard work for both the student and the teacher. It requires an unwavering dedication to perfect reading practices every day in every classroom. The teaching must be uniformly on target, thorough, and persistent. Of utmost importance, in order for the at-risk student to learn to read and be accelerated in his progress, he must do the work of reading himself and read more than other students at this grade placement.

At-risk students should be taught about reading twenty-five percent of the time and do the work of reading seventy-five percent of the time.

In a traditional basal lesson, a teacher spends a great deal of time talking about the reading material and then asks questions about the material after the students have read it. Rather than practicing reading after the instructional lesson, students complete workbook pages, worksheets, or tests. As a result of a careful review of the literature, the authors of *Becoming a Nation of Readers* concluded that the amount of time spent working on workbook pages and skill sheets activities is unrelated to growth in reading.

Educators in classrooms, publishing companies, and universities reviewed the research that pointed out the small amount of time children spend reading. As a result and in an attempt to introduce more reading into the classroom, many districts throughout the nation implemented the Whole Language philosophy. The hope was that students would spend more time reading and developing a love for reading.

A typical course of study in a Whole Language classroom often follows this type of pattern: In a unit on oceans, the teacher reads to the students; the students view a video; they produce an art project; the teacher displays appropriate objects; the students write about vacations at the ocean; they take a field trip to the ocean or an aquarium to study ocean habitation; they cook and sample seafood; they talk about the endangered ocean environment; they locate oceans on a world map; and they invite a speaker to talk with them about ocean-related jobs or commerce.

All of these activities are designed to build a background of knowledge, to make a correlation to various courses of study such as science, social studies and art; to expand the student's receptive vocabulary; and to create an interest so the student will read more about the topic on his own.

The major omission in this scenario is the student doing the work of reading. The teacher is performing an exemplary job, but she is doing all the work for the student. She is teaching her students about reading, but the students are not doing the work of reading. Learning to read and increasing reading abilities comes only with practice. Students must engage in the act of reading.

When at-risk readers come to school, they are already behind their peers in literacy knowledge. In order for at-risk readers to learn to read alongside their peers, they must receive larger amounts of more intense instruction than is normally available. Students must be taught at the instructional level, and then they must be given many opportunities to read at the independent level. During the instructional lesson as well as all other learning activities designed to teach reading, the teacher teaches students how to read twenty-five percent of the time and has the student practice what she has taught him seventy-five percent of the time. How is such a feat accomplished?

Avoid wasting time on unnecessary activities.
At-risk readers are behind in their reading abilities when they enter school. Because of their at-risk factors, at-risk students require more intense, on-target instruction and more practice to make normal progress. In order for them to keep pace with their peers and read at their grade placement level, the instruction must be accelerated and intensified, and they must be given numerous opportunities to practice reading. All of this must be accomplished within the confines of the normal school day. Time is precious. It cannot be squandered.

Though school days now are longer than ever, teachers are faced with an increased workload of instruction. Teachers are responsible for imparting knowledge on art, music, physical education, spelling, handwriting, math, health, social studies, science and technology. They are also expected to provide preventive education in a number of areas addressing social problems, positive action, cultural awareness, sexual abuse, physical abuse, drug education, sex education. They must administer scoliosis checks and develop and practice entertainment programs for the community. The list is endless.

No wonder teachers say they have no time for reading instruction. A Guided Reading Lesson directed by the teacher — teaching at-risk students at their instructional level — is a forty-five minute commitment. It is intense, time-consuming work. And it is the responsibility of the administration to make available the time and the organization for teachers to teach reading to all of the students.

The administration is also responsible for making sure that the reading time is guarded and protected from outside pressures. The community at large puts pressure on the educational community to address numerous social issues in addition to academics. Yet how is the educational community judged?...by the test scores and the academic progress of its students.

So it is the teacher's task and the administration's responsibility to examine every planned activity to determine its academic significance. At-risk students do not have time to watch a movie at school, even if it is the class reward for good behavior. Two hours every Friday before a television screen viewing a movie multiplied by thirty-two weeks is sixty-four hours. Can you sacrifice twelve, five-hour school days?

The educational community is the only segment of society set aside to teach academics to students. The focus cannot be lost. If the student does not become a good reader when he is in the primary grades, there is never again any time set aside to teach him to read.

Never waste time on unnecessary activities.

Learning activities designed for the at-risk student must require him to practice good reader strategies, the skills used by fluent readers.

When at-risk students enter school, they are already behind their peers in literacy development. Because of their at-risk factors, they are more likely to become confused about the reading process once formal reading instruction begins. They also need more intensive reading instruction and more reading practice to make the same amount of progress as their peers.

At-risk readers do not have the luxury of participating in a come-and-go-and-do-and-be program. Nor do they have the time to receive their reading instruction in a highly structured setting that only teaches one of the three cueing systems. Every time they read, they must practice using all the good reader skills.

When a student is reading and he comes to a word he does not know, he can decode the unknown word by using meaning (semantics), structure of the printed language (syntax), or sound/symbol correspondence (graphemics). These three cueing systems are interrelated. A good reader must use all of them with flexibility, automatically choosing the most efficient strategy as he reads. Rarely is one of the cueing systems used in isolation. Rather, the three cueing systems are used in varying combinations. In order to accelerate the at-risk reader in his use of good reader skills, every learning activity must provide practice in all three cueing systems.

The Cut-up Story (Described in Chapter 8) is designed to build a perfect, practiced understanding of the concept of print. It gives the student the structure of language at the student's instructional level and teaches the graphemics of print in a meaningful context. It develops efficient eye movement and improves deficiencies in the student's oral language. It supplies the teacher with appropriate reading material so she can teach the student at his instructional level. Cut-up Stories provide an additional, personal benefit, as well, for not only has the student authored the story, but it also becomes a book he owns and keeps in his home.

The Read Together (Described in Chapter 9) increases the student's receptive vocabulary and broadens his base of experience. It teaches tracking, directionality, return sweep, and eye teaming. The Read Together develops the student's awareness of the structure of language in print about six months above his instructional reading level. The student reads the story using his memory and his knowledge of graphemics to match the print on the page. During rereadings, the student develops fluency and the ability to read in the voice of the author.

The Guided Reading Lesson increases the student's receptive vocabulary and broadens his base of experiences. The student is taught the word recognition he needs to know in order to read at his instructional level. He practices using these skills in real reading and real writing situations. To accelerate the student's acquisition of the skill, it is taught in a small group using all three modalities. The teacher guides and coaches the student in the use of good reader strategies during the reading and rereading of the story. Observing the student, the teacher identifies and prevents any misconceptions or ineffective reading practices. The Guided Reading Lesson helps the student develop independence in reading, and because the student always uses good reader practices, his reading ability improves every time he reads.

At-risk readers must receive their reading instruction in a small group setting seated at a table with the teacher.

In a typical group of six at-risk readers, all the at-risk factors are represented. Two students might be hyperactive, one has visual memory problems, two have auditory interference and one student may be shy and withdrawn. All six may have a poor background of experience in literacy.

These students are unable to make normal progress in a whole class setting because they possess some type of physical interference that makes learning difficult for them. The hyperactive student cannot attend, so he misses major points. The student with auditory interference processes the information incorrectly or does not hear all of the information. The student with visual memory problems needs extra support to help him remember. And the shy, withdrawn student is so scared and intimidated he cannot bring himself to take a risk.

The number of students in the group should remain small. If the students are all within the same instructional range, they can be taught in a group of six, though in some schools for a variety of reasons, it is necessary to have seven or eight students in a group. Obviously, instructing a larger group of at-risk students is less effective than a smaller, more manageable one. The ultimate aim is to form the smallest group possible with students whose abilities are similar.

The teacher is seated at the table with her small group of students, allowing her to accommodate the at-risk factors of each student. She directs the student with auditory processing problems to look at her face when she is talking and makes her instruction and discussions more understandable for him. She knows immediately how this student interprets the information. If there is confusion, she clears it up on the spot.

Seated with the students, the teacher encourages and supports the shy, timid student, making sure he is engaged in the lesson. She celebrates mistakes with him and helps him understand that good readers take risks and make mistakes.

The teacher makes sure the student with Attention Deficit Disorder is attending, redirecting him when he is not paying attention. She constantly calls him back to the task and helps him persist in doing the work of reading. She takes his finger and helps him point to the words as he is reading. With the teacher's help and constant support, with her focus on directing him to attend to the task at hand, the A.D.D. student can learn to read.

Her position at the table allows the teacher to see everything her at-risk students are doing and affords her the immediate opportunity to clear up confusions quickly while keeping them at the task of reading. Reading at a table also helps the student keep his book steady and always in front of him so that attending to the conventions of print is possible. It sets up a routine the at-risk student can depend on. It makes the teaching of reading serious business. At-risk students cannot make rapid progress in a come-and-do-and-go-and-be atmosphere.

At-risk readers must practice word recognition skills using all three modalities, though the at-risk reader must learn through his strong modality.

This enables him to make rapid progress and to avoid the possibility of developing misconceptions about the reading process. The teacher works within the framework of the small group of at-risk readers where all of the at-risk factors are present.

If all three modalities are used when teaching word recognition skills, the student is able to learn in the small group setting. Initially, each individual student uses his strongest modality to learn the skills he needs in reading. Continued practice helps him develop the ability to use and learn through his weak modality.

In this example, all three modalities are utilized in teaching the sound/symbol correspondence for the letter *l*.

After giving each student a picture of a lion, the teacher says:

This is a lion.

Look at the lion and say its name.

Tell me a story about a lion.

Say the first sound you hear and then say its name.

The teacher then introduces the letter by saying:

This is the letter *l*.

The letter *l* represents the sound you hear at the beginning of the word *lion*.

Say the word *lion*.

What are some other words that look and sound like *lion* at the beginning?

Yes. *lemon, lace, Larry, lip, lazy.*

Say the sound we hear at the beginning of each word:

l- lion

l-lemon

l-lace

l-Larry

l-lip

l-lazy.

Look at the letter. Describe it for me.

Is it a tall letter, an on-the-line letter, or a below-the-line letter?

Yes, it is a tall letter.

 It is long and straight?

What are some things that look like L?

Yes. A pole, a stick, a lamp.

Write the letter on your white board.
Say *l. l-lion.*
Write it again.
It is a tall letter like a pole.
Take your finger and erase the letter. Say the sound as you erase.
Close your eyes. Can you see the letter?
Write the letter with your finger on your arm.
Write the letter with your finger on the table.

Write the letter with your finger on your partner's back while your partner says the sound of the letter.

Have each student write the word using crayon until there is a wax buildup. Have the student run his hand over the *l* as he says the sound and key words. Have him run his hand over the words as he describes the letter. The student can remember the key word *lion*. This helps him isolate the sound represented by *l* at the beginning, or he can remember the visual and link it with the auditory. When he comes to the word *look* in his reading he can say, *l*, like in the words lion and look.

In order to be a good reader and make normal progress the student must become efficient with all the word recognition skills. A good reader does not use only visual analysis or phonetic analysis or meaning as a cue. Good readers use all of the word recognition skills.

Using all three modalities to teach and practice gives the student support as he develops his abilities in each of the word recognition skills.

Chapter Three

What Good Readers Do

When at-risk readers begin school, they are already below their grade placement in literacy development. In order for these students to become good readers functioning at their grade placement, they must make more than one year's progress in the nine month span of a school term.

To close this gap, at-risk readers must be taught more, and they must practice more. They must always practice the skills and strategies used by good readers: they must use meaning to decode; they must anticipate, predict and guess; they must combine meaning cues with visual cues, and they must combine meaning cues with phonic cues; they must use efficient directional movement; they must take risks, use the innate rules of language as they apply to print, and use context to decide if a word is important; they must self-correct. Reading is easy for fluent readers who use these many strategies when reading.

From the outset, a teacher must be careful to make sure students acquire and understand the right concept and ideas about print and that they use the necessary strategies that will make them good readers. The longer students practice misconceptions, the more difficult it is to instill in them and have them consistently use the strategies of good readers. Once they become accustomed to using poor reader strategies, developing and practicing these wrong concepts, the more difficult it becomes to have them make progress and move forward.

Good readers must use meaning to decode. When children begin to learn to read, they must be taught the strategies of good readers. The first good reader strategy is the use of meaning to decode. The reader's eyes must move across print efficiently. He must pick up the graphemic cues — the relationship between sounds and letter shapes — and match them with what he is expecting in the story. When his reading ceases to make sense, he must know that he has to go back and cross check his choice of words, realizing that his predictions are not working.

When a good reader picks up a book, he automatically has certain expectations regarding the contents. As he reads, he is able to anticipate, guess and predict the outcome of the story. His eyes fly across print, reading from left to right with a return sweep, focusing only on about every tenth word. A good reader constantly changes his prediction based on the information in the story.

While it is important for the student to use meaning to decode, he also must use the graphemic cues. So if a student reads, "The rabbit jumped over the fence" from text that is written, "The bunny jumped over the fence," the appropriate response from the teacher is, "Now, let's look at this. I know what you did. You said, 'The rabbit jumped over the fence,' and I can understand what would make you think that. Good readers do use meaning to decode and that certainly would make sense, but what word do we know that means the same as rabbit and starts the way this word starts?" The teacher may need to point to the beginning letter in bunny, direct the student to reread, and ask him to make the sound that b represents at the beginning of a word. The teacher should avoid doing the work for the student, but direct and help the student do the work.

A student who has trouble attending to visual configurations relies too heavily on the use of meaning. He must use meaning in combination with the other good reader strategies. A student who has auditory difficulties does not have the right sounds matched up with the right symbols, so when he reads, "The bunny jumped over the fence," he may read, "The bunny ran over the fence." Using efficient eye movement is difficult for many students. From the outset, they must persist and look at print, and as their eyes move across print they must look at the beginning sounds.

A student must be comfortable with the fact that there may be some things he will not know how to do. He must be able to guess and take risks. Good readers constantly self-correct, know when the meaning does not make sense, or that it makes sense but does not match the graphemic cue. Students who are shy and timid or who have auditory difficulties or who come from poor backgrounds of experience need a great deal of support in order to be able to use meaning to decode.

Structure of Language in Print

In order to be a good reader, a student must have a sense for the innate rules of language as they appear in print. The notion that if a child is able to learn to talk, he should be able to read, or that reading is as natural as learning to talk just is not so. There is much more involved in the act of reading than in the act of talking. Language in print is not the same as spoken language. A student must have knowledge of the structure of language the way it appears in print.

Students to whom books have been read and who have been exposed to print stand a much better chance of developing and becoming good, fluent readers. Students who have not experienced reading in the home have not had an exposure to language the way it appears in print. In order to be a good reader, a student must have a knowledge of the structure of language. Auditory students, even those who have been read to, will have difficulty with the structure of language because of background noise interference or because of chronic ear infections which prevents them from hearing the story when it was read.

Learning activities must provide the background for language as it appears in print, which is extremely different from spoken language: "It's time to get up," said Mom. "Moo, Moo," said the cow. Children who have never had books read to them have not heard the structure of language as it appears in print. They cannot possibly anticipate, guess and predict. Children who have been read to understand more easily how to match the visual cues with the phonetic cues, and consequently they have a sense of what is going to happen in the story simply because they are familiar with the language of print.

What Poor Readers Do

Poor Readers have few strategies. They rely on what can be invented from memory, do not attend to the visual details, do not self-correct, and do not use meaning. Poor readers make random guesses.

Reading is hard work for poor readers. If the poor reader is allowed to practice these ineffective strategies, they become a habit, and the student is labeled a "disabled reader."

When good readers come to words they do not know, they have many strategies which they use interchangeably. When poor readers come to words they do not know, they employ few strategies as they attempt to decode print. Many of them rely on sounding out letters as an aid in decoding unknown words, but the way they sound words out is to say the individual sound for every letter. One student knew all of his letters and could even match up the right sounds with them, but he had terrible problems with reading. He believed the way to read was to say the individual sound for every letter. While it is proper to use phonics, it is not good reader strategy to sound out every letter in an unknown word.

Poor readers often invent the story from memory and tell about what they think would be there, not matching the graphemic details, or they just blindly guess at words. Often times their strategy is to ask someone when they come to a word they do not know. A student will never be an effective, independent reader if his strategy is to ask someone when he comes to a word he does not know. In order to be an effective, good reader a student must have strategies that help him go about decoding print and working on print independently. Poor readers must be made to develop and use the skills good readers use.

Case Study - Laura

Laura has a severe auditory problem. She can visually remember letters, but she cannot link up the sound with them. At the completion of her first grade year, her only skill was knowing that letters made words. When she wrote, her letters were squeezed together, and the letters and sounds that went together did not in any way have anything to do with the words she said were there. Laura's strategy was to either write a story cramming random letters together and then tell that story to her class as if she really were saying the words on the page. When she wanted to "read" a story, she simply had her friend read it to her first, and then she used her memory to tell the story. She did not pay any attention to the actual print and had no word-to-word match.

During the time Laura was receiving instruction in *Early Detection, Necessary Action*, she asked if she could put away the marker she used to keep her focused on the print before her. Indeed, she had advanced to a point at which her eye movement was efficient, and the marker was no longer necessary. Without the marker, Laura covered her eyes with her hands, peeking through one finger as she looked at the words before her. She read a little bit and then she closed her eyes and told the story. I asked, "Laura, what are you doing?" She said, "I'm trying to read without my eyes." That is exactly what she had been doing all along. She would have someone read a book to her and use her memory to tell the story, paying absolutely no attention to the print on the page.

Laura is an excellent example of a student who has developed many misconceptions about print and once they have developed these misconceptions, they continue to practice them. The longer they practice them, the more ingrained they become, and every time they are taught something new, they simply take their misconceptions and incorporate them into what the teacher is teaching.

Reading is hard work for poor readers. The longer they practice inefficient strategies, the more the strategies become habitual and the more difficult it is to break them. It is imperative from the beginning to make sure students are developing the right concepts of print. The learning activities of *Early Detection, Necessary Action* ensure and insist that students practice good reader strategies.

Learning to read is easy for students who do not have at-risk factors. For students who have at-risk factors, learning to read is extremely difficult. Often times these students put forth enormous effort, but because of something that interferes with their ability to get a good understanding of print, they develop the wrong concept and reading becomes tedious. Think of the students who come to school and everything is easy for them. They get all the rewards. They get to do the extra errands for the teacher, they get good notes sent home, they get constant praise.

At-risk students who have reading difficulties come to school and work hard, but because their problems are often not diagnosed or are incorrectly diagnosed, their misconceptions are compounded rather than eliminated, and none of their hard work pays off. They never get any praise, they never get the personal reward that comes from knowing they are learning and making progress. Learning to read, therefore, becomes laborious, and they develop a distaste for it.

There are certain elements that learning activities must include in order for students to develop good reader strategies. Learning activities must provide students with the background information and meaning words they will encounter in their reading. Learning activities must require students to look at and practice learning print in the right way. Students must practice using efficient directional movement. At-risk students must be taught in a small group, and the learning activities must cover all the modalities. At-risk students must be taught with real books which encourage them to practice using meaning, anticipation, and guessing to decode.

The objective of *Early Detection, Necessary Action* is to never let students get confused. It assures that they are seeing print in the right way, that they have the right concept about print, and that every time they work on print, they use the skills good readers use.

Chapter Four

Guided Reading Lesson: Tell Them Everything They Need to Know

The Guided Reading Lesson is specifically designed for at-risk readers, and it is the platform which allows students to use and constantly practice the reading strategies that good, fluent readers use. Early Detection Necessary Action students are taught a Guided Reading Lesson daily under the direct supervision of a trained teacher. Based on the idea that the coach — the reading teacher — must tell them everything they need to know, their reading ability constantly improves.

The technique of the Guided Reading Lesson builds a bridge to the student's prior knowledge and strengthens his connection to the story. It is the learning activity where students are taught to use all of their knowledge at their instructional level — that is, for every 100 words they read, they miss no more than ten — allowing the teacher to see what they do when they come to a word they do not know.

Pre-reading activities — telling the student everything he needs to know, building a bridge of knowledge in order to strengthen his connection with the story, and broadening the experiences of the student so that he is able to call upon those experiences to anticipate and decode using meaning — are the cornerstones of the Guided Reading Lesson.

The Guided Reading Lesson is taught four times weekly for a period of forty-five minutes each session. In this activity, students learn to read books that are at their instructional level. Good coaches train athletes to visualize, to rehearse mentally and to practice before an event. Good reading coaches thoroughly prepare students for reading by providing them with visual images of the story: the characters, vocabulary, setting, and structure.

For at-risk readers, it is vital to *tell them everything they need to know* so that reading the story will be easy and so that they can use meaning as well as graphemics (sound/symbol correspondence) to decipher the unknown word. This is called decoding. Reading takes little effort for fluent readers because they have background information. The process of telling them everything they need to know gives at-risk readers a foundation for the story and enables them to anticipate and use meaning as they read, the skills a student must use in order to be a fluent reader.

In telling them everything they need to know, you should attempt to activate their prior knowledge. Ask questions that relate them personally to the book. Introduce them to vocabulary words in the story, provide a setting for the story, and highlight the function words and the structure of the sentences. Based on the information you have supplied, give them an opportunity to predict. Introduce them to aspects of grammar used within the story.

These criteria must be met in all pre-reading activities:
- Tell the students everything they need to know.
- Activate their prior knowledge.
- Provide knowledge about the characters, setting and any action that takes place.

In teaching reading, you must tell your students everything they need to know in order to practice doing what good readers do...guess and predict accurately.

After the pre-reading activity in which you have told them everything they need to know, the students read the story silently. If this is a difficult concept, tell them to read the story in their heads. Working on their own develops independent readers and gives the students time to practice and work at the skills fluent readers use.

If a student is having difficulty with a word, avoid telling him the word. Rather, encourage him and give appropriate clues and guidance so he can decipher it on his own. Silent reading gives the student the opportunity to learn to help himself over reading hurdles. If he reads the book too quickly, tell him to read it quietly in your ear while the other students are reading silently. You must make him stay on task and insist that he read the book.

During oral reading, coach the students to self-correct. Self-correcting allows the student to monitor his own reading and to hear how the meaning does not make sense when he guesses incorrectly. Good reading coaches reinforce self-correction and give suggestions and clues to build competence and confidence in their students. As each student reads orally, the teacher makes note of what the student does when he comes to a word he does not know, and she adjusts the instruction to meet the needs of the student.

Teach them the cueing system that good readers use. Does it make sense? Does it sound right? Does it look right? Before long, the students will understand that meaning, grammar, and graphemics (sound/symbol correspondence) play a major role in decoding the print before them.

The Guided Reading Lesson is a sequential introduction of skills which enables the student to progress through the emergent reader stage to a point at which he is reading fluently by the time he advances to the first hardback primer level. You are teaching him to use all the knowledge available to him at his instructional level, the level at which you are able to see what he does when he comes to a word he does not know.

During the Guided Reading Lesson, the goal is to teach twenty-five percent of the time and have the student read seventy-five percent of the time. He must practice reading in order to become a reader. He must be kept on task. He must attend to the print before him. He must do the work of reading. It is the only way to learn to read. Do not ever excuse him from reading or send him away for misbehaving. This is exactly what he wants you to do. Reading is hard work, and many at-risk students will do everything in their power to flee from this difficult task. Do not allow this to happen.

Start with a warm-up activity. Re-read a book you have already taught, a favorite book or one the students have chosen, or a cut-up story as described in Chapter 8. Review a skill they were taught during the initial reading of the book.

Introduce them to the new book by giving the story background. Talk about the vocabulary. There will be words they do know and words they do not know. Activate their prior knowledge by relating information in the story with experiences they may have had or have heard about. Analyze the words in the story. What do they mean? What do they look like? Have they heard the word before? Give them everything they need in order to decode the story, but do not read the story. Give them enough background to decode the ten percent they do not know, to be able to anticipate, guess, and predict, and to practice good reader skills. Tell them everything they need to know so that when they come to a word they do not know, they can figure it out. These steps help make them independent readers.

The teacher's task during the Guided Reading Lesson is to supply the students with all the information they need for them to practice reading and decoding unseen print.

In teaching students to guess and predict, it is important to give them the opportunity to say what they think or understand. When students attempt to make predictions, they become actively involved in reading. It is not as important to be right as it is for them to be motivated enough to start wondering what the story is about. This is how they become actively involved in the process of reading. The mere act of guessing — right or wrong — gets them involved. That is what good readers do. As they read, ask them if they want to re-evaluate their guess. Stop midway through and ask if they would like to change their guess. Eventually, the student will involve himself in this exercise without your assistance. You must constantly stress what good readers do. Guessing is one of the strategies good readers use.

Just as guessing helps increase awareness of print and what it has to say, so does visualizing aid comprehension by making characters, setting and actions seem more real. At-risk readers do not visualize. Nothing pops into the mind of an at-risk reader. Good readers visualize. Tell your students to close their eyes and ask them what they see. This exercise helps them to see with their minds. Walk them through it and then give them practice doing it. The more guidance students receive in the early stages of the reading experience, the sooner they will be able to decode independently. You need to make it easy for them so they will want to do it and be successful at it. You must engineer the principles of reading so that they will choose to do it.

The process, therefore, of the Guided Reading Lesson is this:

Begin with a warm-up time. Re-read a previously taught book which the teacher has chosen or which the students have selected. Review or teach a skill from this book.

Present a new book through pre-reading activities including vocabulary development. Introduce them to the structure of language and of print. Connect what they know to what is new, activating their prior knowledge. Encourage them to predict and anticipate what might happen next. Advise them to take risks, to guess. Constantly work on improving their oral language.

The next step is Word Analysis where the student makes a connection from his head to print. He reinforces his knowledge of the sight words he knows and builds his sight word list by learning new ones. Teach word recognition skills, combining visual, kinesthetic and auditory methods.

Since you have thoroughly discussed the book and have told them everything they need to know, now ask them to read silently inside their heads. Encourage persistence. Be aware that many children will flip through the pages and pronounce the book read. You must keep them on task, and if a student finishes the book quickly, have him read it quietly in your ear.

Silent reading enables the student to understand that the task of reading is between him and the book. He must learn how to decode the words himself without the teacher's assistance. Avoid telling him the words, but coach him through the strategies of good readers including how to decode using meaning, context and sound/symbol correspondence.

Silent reading is followed by oral reading. Always model good reader strategies. Constantly ask them what it is good readers do when they come to a word they do not know. Students should point to each word with their index finger until they are able to attend to print. You cannot expect them to read with fluency, phrasing, and expression at this point. For the teacher, oral reading is diagnostic time. Listen for what they do when they come to a word they do not know. Coach them through using the skills that good readers use. Ask them to go back and re-read the sentence and say the beginning sound of the words they do not know. Give all the support they need, but do not tell them the word. If the student still cannot figure it out, make a notation of that word. Review that word the next day in the Guided Reading Lesson. Direct students to practice connecting the meaning of a word to a visual clue as well as to a sound clue. Ask them to reread, helping them persist in decoding the book. Recognize and congratulate the good reader strategies they use, and always make sure they are reading at their instructional level, not above or below it.

By this point in the Guided Reading Lesson, the students should have spent seventy-five percent of the time reading and practicing the skills you have taught.

The Write Every Day activity which closes the Guided Reading Lesson teaches students how writing is connected to reading. Writing is the process of linking up what is in their heads with the symbols and putting it on paper. It is important to see the connections students make from their heads to print, invaluable information for the teacher to know where they are in their acquisition of print. Since print is not flexible, having the students write everyday helps you understand what they are seeing when they look at print.

The Guided Reading Lesson is a concentrated learning activity and one of the most important. Reading is intense work for both the student and the teacher. It often is tempting to allow other things to interfere. If you acknowledge the overwhelming influence of reading in everything you do as a teacher as well as in the student's daily life, you automatically understand the importance of the time and effort you expend every day in teaching reading. Never lose sight of the fact that students cannot learn or excel at any other subject if they cannot read.

The following is a detailed description of the Guided Reading Lesson.

Review & Warm-up

In the review of the previous story, students may choose to select a favorite book and read it silently. The teacher may direct them to read the book she taught them the day before. The teacher may teach again a skill or vocabulary words that troubled the students on the previous day, and then let them read the book. The teacher may have the students read to each other, or go around the group and have each student read his favorite part of a particular book. The students may read the Read Together (Described in Chapter 9) that was taught earlier in the week.

The purpose of the review of a previous story is to let the students have time to practice and to use previously taught skills. For beginning, emergent readers, just getting the extra practice of reading material that is familiar to them is reason enough to do this portion of the lesson.

The reading of a previous book is also a good time for emergent readers to work on skills they would not have in the first reading of a book at their instructional level: the skills of fluency, reading with expression, and reading in the author's voice.

Students who have not been read to or who have not had an enriched background of experience have a limited vocabulary and are not familiar with the structure of language the way it appears in print. A student who has visited a zoo or understands what a safari is might be able to decipher a book about large game animals. But a student who has not had those experiences will not have the same level of knowledge.

The teacher approaches the reading of a book about large game animals by first showing her students the illustrations and names of the animals pictured in the book. She teaches the sight word *the* and then lets the students read the story silently. "The lion, the zebra, the rhinoceros... ." The student is unable to read the animal names anywhere but in the context of the known book. On the rereading during the review, he does not learn the animal names as sight words. He learns *the* as a sight word. He uses his knowledge of graphemics to form the beginning sound of the animal and matches that with the illustration and meaning to decode.

The rereading of known books gives the student a schemata in his mind for large game animals. Every time he rereads the book, he pronounces the animal name, sees the animals in their habitat, and connects these animals with the zoo or a safari in their natural habitat.

On another day, the teacher teaches a readiness book about farm animals: "one cow; two pigs; three horses; four chickens." The student rereads the book during the review and during independent reading. He learns the words as sight words. Now he has a schemata for farm animals and is able to make the distinction between farm animals and large game animals. Later, when he is taught a book about ocean animals, his knowledge and experience is expanded even further.

So even though this student has not been to a zoo or does not live in a rural area where farm animals abound or has never visited the ocean, he has read about animals who inhabit these places and his background of experience is strengthened. The many repetitions — and it takes many repetitions — of naming the animals, of saying the words in the context of meaning gives the student the experience of becoming familiar with these animals.

The rereading and repetition also provide the student with the structure of language as it appears in print. Every time he rereads or hears a classmate reread, he becomes more familiar with book talk: the language that, to this point, has been so foreign to him.

The review and rereading of known books plays a significant role in the quest to accelerate the at-risk reader. Keep in mind that the at-risk reader is already behind in his literacy development when he comes to school. If he is ever going to read grade placement material, he must make more than standard progress. He must be accelerated in his literacy knowledge.

The teacher may want to review a skill during the review of known books. For example, during the first oral reading, the teacher notices the students are having difficulty with the dialogue word, *yelled*. The text reads, "Hey, come on, yelled the children." The students interpret the word as *yellowed*.

The teacher says, "When the author wants to let us know how the character is talking or communicating in a story, what are some words he could use?" The students might respond with the words *said, cried, whispered, screamed, yelled.* The teacher recites an example using the word that fits the story: "The house is on fire," yelled Dad. Then she instructs the students to reread the page in the book where the word *yelled* is used, and she might say, "What word did the author use? *yelled*? Now read page seven and look for the dialogue word the author uses on that page. Maggie, read the third paragraph and let's all listen for the dialogue word."

During the review of known books, the teacher reviews the skill and has the students practice the skill when they are reading. The practice of the skill is designed in such a way that all the students must do the work of reading to complete the practice.

The time students spend rereading books or reading books that are easy for them counts as real reading and should be included in the goal of having students read seventy-five percent of the time. The additional twenty-five percent of the lesson time is spent teaching the students about reading.

Word Analysis

The activity where students learn to break words apart and put them back together should take into account all the different learning modalities so that the students can learn through one modality or the other. The lesson should be well thought out, it should be concise, and it should be quick. The word analysis activity should always be taken from the book that is being presented to the students for the first time. The word analysis activity does not count as part of real reading, but is part of the twenty-five percent spent on teaching about reading and should take no more than five minutes.

During the Guided Reading Lesson, the teacher teaches the word analysis skill, and the student practices under the teacher's direct supervision. After the teacher has taught the word analysis activity, students may practice independently during the school day at word analysis centers, during practice time at their desks, or with a learning activity at the computer. Word analysis activities may also be assigned as homework.

Receptive Vocabulary

The teaching of receptive vocabulary is an opportunity to broaden the student's ability to understand language by increasing the number of words to which he knows the meaning. During the receptive vocabulary portion of the Guided Reading Lesson the students are provided with all of the meaning words that are going to appear in the story they are about to read. These are the words the students decode with meaning, rather than with word recognition skills.

The teacher reads through the story and picks out any words the students might have difficulty with because they would not know the meaning. She does not teach meaning words as sight words. This part of the lesson teaches the specific skill of using meaning to decode. She takes the vocabulary words from the story, reviews them and talks about them with the students to make sure they know to expect the words to be in the book.

Pre-reading Activities

Following the receptive vocabulary development, the teacher directs the pre-reading activities by introducing the characters in the story. She tells the students the names of the characters; makes them familiar with any action that is going to take place; talks about the setting; encourages them to visualize what is going to be happening in the story; activates their knowledge and finds out what they already know about and can relate to the story; sets a purpose for reading; and then directs them to read the story silently. The teacher is prepared for the fact that students will make noises as they read silently. They will mumble, move their lips, and whisper as they read. This behavior is acceptable. Silent reading means working on print alone, using and practicing good reader skills on previously unseen and unheard print.

Silent Reading

During the silent reading portion of the Guided Reading Lesson, the teacher makes sure the students are persisting and staying on task. She watches over each student as they read to make sure they are attending to the print. She goes from student to student and says, "Read a little bit of this to me" or "When I read this story I... ." She keeps them actively involved. When a student turns to the back of the book and finishes too fast, the teacher redirects him and says, "Well, let's read this again."

At-risk students take a great deal of encouragement, support, and meticulous watching over to make sure they really are reading during the silent reading portion. As difficult as the concept of silent reading is to students, it is extremely important that the students do read silently, for this is how independent readers are developed. This is the exercise that enables students to know they can read and that they have their own strategies for reading. Therefore, never read the story aloud to the children. Always direct them to read it first.

Oral Reading

Oral reading follows silent reading. Oral reading is an opportunity for the teacher to look for what the student does when he comes to a word he does not know. She uses the coaching chart, *When You Come To a Word You Don't Know, Don't Let It Bug You.*

Every student must read some portion of the book orally to the teacher who coaches him through using good reader strategies. If the student comes to a word he does not know, the teacher says, "Let's go back and reread that sentence. Now let's reread it and say the first sound. What word would make sense here?" If the child still cannot decipher the word, she encourages him to read on to the end of the sentence and has him internalize the idea that when he comes to a word he does not know, he can reread it and say the first sound and just guess at a word that would make sense. This approach only works if students are reading material at their instructional level.

As the teacher coaches, supports and helps one student, the other students get the benefit of hearing the individualized instruction. In addition, the oral reading time provides an opportunity to teach reading group etiquette: "Jeremy, I saw that you knew the word Sally was struggling with, and I really appreciate that you didn't tell her. You gave her time to do what good readers do and get the practice of figuring out the word by herself. That's really what we're all doing. So, Jeremy, I really appreciate that, and when you come to a word you don't know, we're going to make sure we give you time to figure it out."

This type of response also says it is okay for Sally not to know a word. It is, in fact, an expectation that all of the students will come to words they do not know, and that all students will have an opportunity to be able to work at those words and figure them out.

It is during the exercises of silent reading and oral reading that students acquire the skills necessary to become independent readers, skills which encourage them to choose to read on their own. Without these skills, at-risk students will never accept reading as an independent activity. Rather, reading will be an activity in which they participate only at the teacher's insistence.

Write Every Day
 The Write Every Day activity as it is connected to reading is different than the traditional concept of writing. This is not the type of writing that relays a burning message. This is not writing for fluency. This is a written response to the material the student has just read. The Write Every Day activity is designed to help the student make a connection between reading and writing. It helps him hear the sounds that go with the different symbols; it enables him to exercise the right concepts of print while he is writing; and it assures the teacher that his response to the story demonstrates an understanding and comprehension of what he has read.

The goal of the Guided Reading Lesson is to teach students about reading twenty-five percent of the time and to have them do the work of reading seventy-five percent of the time. It is easy to reverse those time elements, for teachers are such good workers that they often end up doing all the work. Teachers cannot do the work of reading for the students. Students must do the work of reading themselves.
 It is extremely important that teachers keep the teaching of reading to twenty-five percent of the time, and that under the teacher's watchful, careful guidance, the students spend seventy-five percent of that time in the act of reading, practicing what the teacher has taught them.
 The parts of the Guided Reading Lesson which count as real reading are the review of the previous story, the silent reading, the oral reading, and the writing every day. The other portions of the Guided Reading Lesson teach children about reading. Be careful to spend the right amount of time with students actively involved in the real act of reading.

Guided Reading Lesson for At-Risk Students
 The following is a narrative of a Guided Reading Lesson beginning with the review of a previous book. The books referred to in this example of a Guided Reading Lesson are *Little Pig, Baby Gets Dressed,* and *Let's Have a Swim*, all published by The Wright Group. The reading level of each book is at the second pre-primer level. The teacher is seated at a table with her six at-risk readers. The teacher is using a book at the students' instructional level, a book they can read with

ninety percent accuracy. The teacher must provide the students with all the information they need so they can practice using good reader skills as they decode the extra ten percent. Keep in mind that the students are unable to read the new title without the teacher's help. The students should be doing the work of reading seventy-five percent of the time during the Guided Reading Lesson.

Review of a known book:
To the teacher
- Watch all students closely, keeping them on task, redirecting, encouraging and giving clues as needed.

Say:

1. We are going to read Let's Have a Swim!
2. Can you name one animal we will read about?
3. Tell your partner the name of the animal you have in mind.
4. Now read the book inside your head.
5. Remember to do what good readers do as you are reading.

- During the first oral reading, you observe that Jeremy says *jump* instead of *jumped*. Being a diagnostic teacher, you take this opportunity to make sure Jeremy is not practicing disabling reading strategies.

Say:

1. Jeremy, read the book in my ear.
2. Remember to pronounce the endings when you are reading.
3. This is the word jumped.
4. Good readers always pronounce all of the word.
5. Students, open your books to page two.
6. Jeremy, read page two aloud.
7. I liked the way you gave close attention to the word jumped. I heard ed at the end.
8. Scott, read page four.
    Scott: "The hippopotamus jumped in."
    "The giraffe jumped in."
    "Let's have a swim!"
9. Put your finger under the word hippopotamus.
10. Say the word.
11. Put your finger under the word giraffe.

12. Say the word.
13. Maggie, please read page six.
    Maggie: "The zebra jumped in."
    "The elephant jumped in."
    "Let's have a swim!"
14. Let's read the animal names on page six: zebra, elephant.
15. Tim, page eight, please.
    Tim: "The alligator jumped in."
16. Tim, I know what made you call that word alligator. The picture looks like an alligator and alligators do swim. Look at this word. What animal would make sense and also begin like this word begins?
    Tim: crocodile
    "The crocodile jumped in."

- Make sure students develop a perfect, practiced understanding of print.
- They should understand that print is not flexible.
- They should use all three cueing systems when they read.

17. Let's read the rest of the book together.

    - Make sure the students read with proper phrasing, fluency, and in the voice of the author.

18. Start at page two and read all of the animal names aloud: buffalo; baboon; hippopotamus; giraffe; zebra; elephant; crocodile; buffalo; baboon; hippopotamus; giraffe; zebra; elephant; crocodile.

    - Vocabulary categorizing jungle animals.

19. Where do these animals live?
    Students: These animals live in the jungle.
20. You are one hundred percent correct. I'm glad crocodiles don't live here!

Word Analysis

To the teacher:
- Materials needed: alphabet cards s, h, e, e, p, f, t, l, m, b, p.

Say:

1. This is the word sheep.
2. Say the word.
   Students: sheep
3. What two letters represent the sound you hear at the beginning of the word?
   Students: sh
4. Say the word. Make the word sheep using your letters.
   - Teach the new skill: words having double e usually have the long e sound.
   - Review sh, st, fl - initial and final consonant replacement.
5. Say the word and listen for the sound the vowels represent. What sound do you   hear?
   Students: e
6. The sound ee represents is the long sound for e. It says its name.
7. Place your finger under the two vowels in the word.
8. Look at the word. What do you see?
   Students: sheep.
9. What sound do you hear?
   Students: the long e
10. That is the sound for the long e. When two e's are together in a word, the e usually has the long e sound.
11. Look at your letters. Can you write the word beep?
12. Say the word. What sound do the double es make?
    Students: beep. the long e sound.
13. Can you write the word peep? Say the word.
14. Now write the word steep. What two letters blend together to make the sound at the beginning of the word steep? st.
15. Now I am going to try to trick you. Listen to this word: feet.
16. Say the word. What sound do you hear at the beginning of the word?
    Students: feet. f.

17. Yes, like in fish. Where would you put the letter f in the word feet?
18. Say the word and listen for the sound at the end of the word. What would do you hear at the end?
19. Can you place the letter t in the correct place in the word feet?
20. Let's do the same exercise with the words sleet, fleet, sheep.
21. Place your finger under the vowels.
22. Look at the word.
23. Say the word.
24. What sound do you hear in the middle of the word?
    Students: the long e.

Vocabulary Development

To the teacher:
- categorizing farm animals
- review plurals
- attending to endings, words
- review the suffix er

Say:
1. Today we are going to read a story about a little pig and other farm animals. Can you name animals we would expect to find on a farm? I will write them on the board.
    Students: cows, horses, chickens, pigs, ducks, sheep, goats, roosters.
2. Yes. These are animals we would find on a farm.
3. Listen as I read them to you.
4. Did you hear the s at the end of some words?
5. Read the names of these farm animals with me. The first word is cows. The s added to the word cow means there is more than one cow. When we read names of the farm animals, make sure we use our good reader skills and say the s at the end.
    Teacher & Students: cows, horses, chickens, pigs, ducks, sheep, goats, roosters.
6. Now you read the names of the farm animals as I point to them.
7. Great. I heard the s at the end of the words.
8. This is the word painter. Say the word. What does a painter do?
    Students: A painter paints - cars, houses, pictures.

9. Yes. A painter is a person who paints.
10. This is the word wrestler. Say the word. What does a wrestler do?
    Students: A wrestler wrestles or fights someone.
11. Yes. A wrestler is a person who wrestles.
12. This is the word butcher. Do you know what a butcher does?
    Students: A butcher cuts.
13. A butcher is a person who cuts meat. The grocery store has butchers who cut the meats and package them to sell.
14. Say these words with me: painter, wrestler, butcher.
15. What do you hear at the end of each word?
    Students: er
16. paint - painter; farm - farmer; play - player; walk - walker.
17. When er is added to the end of these words it means a person who does.

Pre-reading

To the teacher:
- Place, setting, characters, action
- Predicting, anticipating, guessing, visualizing
- Set a purpose

Say:
1. The name of this story is <u>Little Pig</u>. Little pig lives on a farm with the other farm animals. Little pig gets bored being at home so he digs out of his home and runs away.
2. What do you think will happen to little pig when he runs away?
    Students: He will get lost.
                   He will get hungry.
                   He will get homesick.
3. I want all of you to close your eyes and see one thing you think will happen to little pig.
4. Do you know you just did another thing good readers do? Good readers always guess and think about the story before they read. The great thing about guessing is   you don't have to be correct and you get to change your guess anytime.
    - Encouraging, supporting.

Failure Is Not An Option

5. I want you to read the story inside your head. While you are reading, I want you to find out two things: The first is why little pig is afraid of the butcher, and the second is what the butcher does with the sausages. Tell me the two things we are going to find out.
   • Setting a purpose.
   Students: Why little pig is afraid of the butcher.
   What the butcher does with the sausages.

Silent Reading

To the teacher:

- Remember the students will mumble the words, move their lips, and sometimes real aloud to themselves. This behavior is okay.
- Remind them that reading silently means doing the work by themselves.
- Monitor the students as they read inside their heads.
- Move from student to student, giving clues if they get stuck.
- Help them persist and stay at the task if they are not reading.
- Remind them quietly about what good readers do.

Oral Reading

To the teacher:

- Reviewing good reader skills
- Coaching self-correcting

Say:

1. Jeremy, read page two. What is one thing you can try if you come to a word you don't know?
   Jeremy: I can reread the sentence and think about a word that would make sense. "Go <u>horse</u>," said the.... "Go home," said the <u>chicken</u>.
   home   hen

"No," said little pig.
2. Jeremy, I like the way you reread the sentence and figured out the word home.
3. How did you know that word was not horse?
    - Helping attend to the graphemics of print.
    Jeremy: It did not sound right.
4. Jeremy, read the sentence again and look at the word you called chicken. Chicken would make sense, but could that word be chicken?
    Jeremy:hen. The word does not begin with c.
5. Scott, please read page three.
    Scott: "Go home," the <u>duck</u> said. "No," said Little Pig.
    ducks
6. Scott, look at the word duck.
    Scott: Oh, that is ducks. That word has an s at the end.
7. Scott, I am so pleased you noticed the s. You should be proud of yourself. I am so impressed with each of you.
    - Developing motivation.
    - Reminding students that when a classmate comes to a word he does not know, give him time to figure it out.
    - It is important for everyone to get practice figuring out words.
8. Lisa, please read page four.
    Lisa: "Go home," said the cows. "No," said Little Pig.
9. Lisa, how did you know that word was the word said?
    Lisa: That is the word authors use to let us know someone is talking.
10. Tim, please read page seven.
    Tim: "Go home," said the butcher, "or I'll make you into <u>summer</u>."
    sausage
11. Tim, please read the last part. Could this word be summer?
    Tim: It begins with s.
12. You are correct, but read the sentence again. Does it make sense with the word   summer? Can you think of a word that would make sense?
    - Helping students persist even when they cannot decode the unknown word.

Tim: I know they look like hot dogs, but I can't think of the word.
13. Well, we won't worry about that word right now. Do you have to know all the words?
Tim: yes.
14. No. You won't know all the words. I make mistakes, your parents make mistakes, and you will make mistakes. When you come to a word you don't know, don't let it bug you.
- During the review of the book the next day, talk about the meat a butcher gets from a pig, and let the students read that part of the book again.

Write Every Day

To the teacher:

- Comprehension
- Inferential sequence of events

Say:
1. Why was Little Pig afraid of the butcher?
    Students: He was so big.
    He did not want to be sausage.
    A butcher could make him sausage.
2. Everyone, find page eight. Read this page aloud to me.
    Students: "Yes, I will," said Little Pig.
3. Little Pig goes back home at the end of the story. Now that Little Pig is back home, what do you think he will tell his mom?
    - Having students reflect on what has been read.
    Students: I am sorry I ran away.
    I played with the other animals.
    I got homesick and the butcher made me cry.
    - Oral language development.
4. On your wipe-off boards, write the one thing you think Little Pig will do when he gets home. What are some things we need to remember when we write?
    - Matching in their heads each phoneme to the correct symbol and transferring it to paper.
    Students: Leave some space after each word.

Take time to work on each word.
I can't write the word butcher.
5. When you try to write butcher, I will help you. That is why I am here. If you knew how to write all the words, you wouldn't need a teacher!
   - Move from student to student, giving clues and support when it is needed.
   - Help students discover what they know and help them take time to transfer that knowledge to print.
   Student: How do you write sorry?
6. Say the word. What do you hear at the beginning?
   Student: sorry. s?
7. Yes. Write the first letter. Now say the word. What do you hear in the middle of the word?
   Student: r.
8. Good. Write what you hear in the middle. Great, Jeremy. What letter makes that sound in the middle of the word sorry?
   Jeremy: r.
9. Look at your r. Make sure it has a curve at the top.
10. Scott, we are not illustrating our sentence. You need to write your sentence. Erase the illustration and I will help you get started. Can you write the word I? Okay. Write that word first. Now say the next word.
    Scott: played.
11. Say it again. What two letters blend together to make the sound at the beginning of played - like plane?
    Scott: pl.
12. Good. Write those two letters. Now work on the rest of the word.
13. Tim, please make your g in the word got a lower case g. Great. thank you!
    - Print is exact; it is not flexible; therefore, make the students practice making perfect connections.
15. Everyone look at your sentence and read it inside your head as you point to each word. Good, now read again and make sure all your sight words are spelled correctly.
16. Scott, look at your word ran. Can you fix the word and make it say ran? Make   sure you don't have a capital letter in the middle of words or at the beginning unless it is someone's name or a place. All of you did a good job with your writing. I

know it is hard work, but you did your writing just the same. You should be proud of yourselves. Do you know why you are such good readers? Yes, because you work so hard. Give yourselves a pat on the back.
- Success is directly related to hard work.
- Develop intrinsic rewards.

After the Guided Reading Lesson, the teacher makes diagnostic notes so she can adjust instruction to match the needs of her students.

Diagnostic Observations:
- Expand students' knowledge about the types of meat that come from pigs.
  pork roast; bacon; sausage; pork chops; ham

Vocabulary Observations:
- Students should reread "Let's Have a Swim" and "Little Pig."
- Make a list of jungle animals and a list of farm animals.
- Students should watch an instructional video during center time about what a butcher does.
- During warm-up of the next lesson, have the students reread "Little Pig" and look for words that use the consonant/vowel pattern: no, go, the.
- Remind the students that when there is one vowel in a syllable and it is the final letter, it usually records its long sound.

Guided Reading Lesson

- Review Previous Story

- Word Analysis

- Receptive Vocabulary

- Pre-reading

- Read Silently

- Read Orally

- Write Every Day

- Practice

When You Don't Know a Word, Don't Let It Bug You!

- Go back to the beginning of the sentence and read the sentence again.

- What would make sense and begin with the first sound?

- If you still aren't sure
    - go back to the beginning of the sentence and read the sentence again.
    - say the first sound, guess, and then read on to the end of the sentence.

- Do good readers know all the words?
    - No! Good readers guess and their guess makes sense.
    - Keep trying.
    - Reread the story.
    - Good readers make mistakes, I make mistakes, your teacher makes mistakes, and you will make mistakes.

- When you don't know a word, don't let it bug you!

E.D.N.A. Observation Checklist
Guided Reading Lesson
(Below Third Grade Reading Level)

Warm-up Time before Guided Reading Lesson
- reread previous book
- reread favorite book
- reread book at direction of teacher
- reviewed or taught a skill from a known book

Word Analysis
- made connections from head to print
- over learned sight words
- built sight words
- word recognition skills
- combined visual, kinesthetic and auditory methods
- word recognition skills taken from student's book

Vocabulary Development and Pre-reading Activities
- connected known to new
- activated prior knowledge
- encouraged predicting
- supported anticipation
- celebrated risk-taking
- previewed characters
- previewed setting
- structure of language
- structure of print
- improved oral language

Silent Reading
- encouraged persistence
- directed students to read inside their heads
- coached students through "What Good Readers Do" when they come to an unknown word

Oral Reading
- modeled good reader strategies
- pointed out and directed students to practice connecting meaning to visual cues

- pointed out and directed students to practice connecting meaning to sound
- directed students to reread
- directed students to reread and skip, then go on to the end of the story
- recognized "good Reader Strategies" used by students
- gave all students an opportunity to use "Good Reader Strategies" when faced with unknown word
- students could read with 90% accuracy
- students persisted and put forth effort to decode unseen book
- students spent 75% of time reading and practicing skills taught by the teacher

<u>Write Every Day</u>
- coached students through writing activity
- supported students while they did the work making connections from head to print
- used writing activity to accelerate students' knowledge of print

E.D.N.A. Observation Checklist
Guided Reading Lesson
(Fourth Grade Reading Level and Higher)

Warm-up
- Reread a specific passage to practice a previously taught skill:
    - word meaning
    - punctuation
    - noting important details
    - noting correct sequence
    - character traits
    - topic of a paragraph
    - main idea of a paragraph
    - other_____

Vocabulary Development and Pre-reading Activities
- connected known to new
- activated prior knowledge
- encouraged prediction
- supported anticipation
- celebrated risk-taking
- previewed characters
- previewed setting
- structure of language
- structure of print
- visualizing

Word Analysis
- combined visual, kinesthetic, and auditory methods
- prefix/suffix/endings
- syllabication
- homographs/homophones
- other_____

Silent Reading
- encouraged persistence
- set a purpose for reading
- coached students through what "Good Readers Do" when they come to an unknown word

Oral Reading
- Read to the end of the sentences:
    - Is it a person, place, or thing?
    - Is it an action word?
    - Does it tell you about something?
    - How many parts are in the word?
    - Say each part in the word.
    - Do you know a word that would make sense?
    - Does it have a prefix or a suffix?
    - Skip the word and read to the end of the sentence.
    - Reread the sentence and keep on reading.
- Students read with 90% accuracy
- Students spend 75% of the time reading.

Write Every Day
- literal recognition or recall
- inference
- evaluation
- appreciation
- context analysis
- reading vocabulary

Chapter Five

Vocabulary Development

Vocabulary is usually classified as having four components which are developed in sequence: listening, speaking, reading and writing. Within the context of the Guided Reading Lesson, at-risk readers develop their reading vocabulary using a variety of activities.

<u>Listening and Speaking Vocabulary</u>

When four- and five-year-old children come to school, they are already able to recognize and respond to thousands of spoken words. For this reason, it is assumed that listening and speaking vocabularies are learned in the home, and reading and writing vocabularies are learned in school.

At-risk students, however, come to school with deficient listening and speaking vocabularies. Since the development of vocabulary occurs in sequence with listening and speaking vocabularies learned first, the school must develop and expand these areas of vocabulary education for the at-risk student in addition to vocabulary development in reading and writing. In order for the at-risk student to make standard progress, both the teacher and the student must be committed to hard work. The at-risk student must receive more intense direct instruction and teacher-directed practice in vocabulary development.

During the pre-reading and vocabulary development stage of the Guided Reading Lesson, provide students with opportunities to expand their listening and speaking vocabularies. Ask students to use the new vocabulary word in the context of an oral sentence and give them many opportunities to relate the new word to known words. Have the students describe a concept orally using the new vocabulary word and then refer to the concept presented by the word in the story. The instruction might sound something like this:

Teacher: This is a story about machines that fly.

	Can you name some machines that fly?
Students:	jet; spaceship; airplane; helicopter.

Teacher:	Look at the illustrations of the helicopter and the jet. Tell me how they are different.

The students respond appropriately.

Teacher:	Explain how they are the same.

The students respond appropriately.

Teacher:	Can anyone add to this explanation?

The students must do the work. Avoid doing all the talking and explaining. Instead, provide direction and information, then elicit language from the students by asking open-ended questions. The student must use the vocabulary in the context of their own spoken language.

<u>Reading Vocabulary</u>

As a student progresses through the school years, he eventually learns to identify and use many written words. Eventually his reading vocabulary will exceed any of the other vocabulary components.

In order to be a good reader, the student must have a large reading vocabulary. A large vocabulary is a solid indication of verbal and mental abilities. Students with large vocabularies have a built-in advantage because they possess superior mental and verbal agility. A student's environment and experiences are crucial in learning concepts and words. A teacher who promotes direct and systematic vocabulary instruction increases the student's reading vocabulary. If enough words from the reading selection are taught in-depth prior to reading, comprehension is facilitated.

For at-risk readers, the teaching of vocabulary words from the reading selection must be more thorough, more intense, and more direct. In other words, tell them everything they need to know. At-risk readers must be told more in order to use good reader skills when they are reading.

Often the concept of telling them everything they need to know is misinterpreted. For instance, in a conference with a classroom teacher, reading specialist, parent, and principal, a student's reading abilities were being discussed. The reading specialist's assessment of the student's reading abilities was higher than that of the classroom teacher. The classroom teacher explained the discrepancy by saying that the reading specialist regularly told the student everything he needed to know in order to read, resulting in a higher assessment of his reading abilities.

The reading specialist was aware that this particular student had two at-risk factors: a severe hearing loss and a poor background of experience. In order for him to use good reader skills — meaning to decode and the ability to anticipate, guess, and predict — the reading teacher knew she had to provide more support and direct teaching. Somehow, the classroom teacher misinterpreted the premise of the Guided Reading Lesson — telling them everything they need to know in order to use good reader skills — as giving them the answers. If the student comes to a meaning word and he cannot read the word, the teacher has not done her job. It is her responsibility to make sure she teaches the student any unknown meaning word before she asks the student to read the story silently. Students must be told everything they need to know.

Attending to word meaning is mandatory when not knowing the word prevents students from understanding the reading selection. The reading selection must be examined by the teacher, and any word the teacher believes might cause confusion must be studied and taught before the student is asked to read the selection.

For example, "The Big Family" written by Joy Cowley is at the primer reading level. Vocabulary development for this story would highlight these words taken directly from the story: shy; celebrate; amusement park; merry-go-round; roller coaster; hoops.

Teacher:
1. These are some words we can expect to find in this story.
2. Let me pronounce them for you.
3. Now pronounce the words with me as we read them together.
4. This is the word shy.
5. If someone is shy, how do they act?
6. Let me make a sentence with the word to help us understand the meaning:
    "When Uncle Ben came to visit, Mary was so shy she always stayed in her room."
7. Can you make a sentence with the word?
8. This is the word celebrate.
9. We always celebrate Scott's birthday.
10. The class will celebrate if we win the attendance award.
11. Read these sentences with me.
12. Can you tell me some things your family likes to celebrate?

The meaning of each word is directly taught and then the students practice using the word in the context of language. In addition to the direct teaching of new vocabulary words, the teacher provides additional meaning cues during the pre-reading activities. The teacher uses a variety of methods to present new vocabulary words to the students, and those methods are discussed later in this chapter.

Word meanings are crucial to the understanding of the printed page. The student needs precise meanings of words, though often the meaning of a word in context is not the same as the individual words that make up the sentence. The word meaning depends on the general context of the sentence.

The following sentences all contain the word cross, but the word cross has quite a different meaning in each sentence.

>   My teacher was cross with me today.
>   I need to cross the street.
>   Mary wears a cross on her necklace.
>   It is not wise to cross my father.

Systematic, planned instruction is needed for growth in the student's receptive vocabulary. Additionally, teachers should take advantage of any situation that provides an opportunity to contribute to the student's vocabulary growth. Vocabulary development should take place during the teaching of all subjects.

Some major points to guide vocabulary development are listed below:
- Teach words in context.
- Teach and discuss key words students will encounter in their reading.
- Teach words systematically and in-depth.
- Teach word meanings through direct experiences whenever possible.
- Use audio/visual aids when direct experience is not possible.
- Understand that at-risk readers need numerous repetitions on the same word.
- Review at-risk readers periodically over long periods of time on the same word.
- Design the vocabulary practice activity so the student must read the reading material to complete the activity, and do this as often as possible.
- Connect what the student knows to the unknown word.

Pre-Reading Strategies

During the pre-reading stage, background information is given, new knowledge is related to existing knowledge, purposes for reading are determined, and significant vocabulary terms are taught. Students use their background knowledge to make predictions about what will happen in the reading selection.

K. D. Wood and N. Robinson, in an article "Vocabulary, Language, and Prediction: A Pre-Reading Strategy" written for The Reading Teacher, formulated pre-reading strategies that supply the students with the vocabulary, the language, and the knowledge to predict outcomes in their reading material. This approach provides a means for pre-teaching vocabulary which uses oral language activities to reinforce each word's structural and semantic characteristics and uses the vocabulary as a basis for predicting what happens in a reading selection.

The steps involved in the Wood and Robinson strategies can be adapted to any story or reading selection. Taking at-risk students through these pre-reading activities gives them practice in and helps them develop the behaviors of a good reader.

A. Vocabulary Preparation

1. The teacher selects which words are more important or those words that will be difficult for the student.

2. The teacher identifies a skill to be taught. The teacher chooses strategies that use these skills in association with the vocabulary word.

3. The selected words are placed on cards, a chart or the board. The teacher presents these words to the students and activates prior knowledge by asking questions to find out what the students think or know about a word.

B. Preparation for Language

1. The teacher asks the student direct questions about structural and conceptual elements of the word. Skill areas identified in part two are practiced and emphasized using the vocabulary words. Following are examples of how the words can be used in specific skill areas:

      a. categorization: Name the animals that live in the jungle.
      b. parts of speech: Which words describe something?
          Which words show action?
          Which words name a person, place or thing?
      c. structural analysis: In which word do you find the sound of i as in life?
      d. synonyms: Which word means the same as large?
      e. antonyms: Which word means the opposite of fast?
      f. context: Give me a sentence with the word clever.
      g. homonyms: What is an entirely different meaning for the word cross?

C. Preparation for Predicting:

1. After the students have an understanding of the vocabulary words, they should be asked to predict what the story will be about, or anticipate what may happen in the story. The student can write the prediction on a board or his paper; he can tell his prediction to someone; the teacher can record the prediction; or the student can just think about his prediction and keep it in his head. The teacher provides many opportunities for the student to re-evaluate his prediction as the reading selection is read.

      a. Setting: Which word tells where Mrs. Trotter lives?
      b. Do you think this story is realistic or is it a fantasy?
      c. Which words give clues about the events in the story?
      d. Reading these words, what type of person do you think Mr. Grump is? Do you think he is a person you want for a friend?

Using this process will build vocabulary. The bonus for the at-risk reader is that it makes him practice the behaviors of the good reader.

Chapter Six

Developing Word Recognition Skills

Good readers use a combination of word recognition skills, applying them automatically. Such skills must be developed and integrated into the reading process so that students learn to use them not in isolation or one at a time, but interchangeably, choosing the most efficient skill in each reading situation. The following is a list of word recognition skills grouped into major categories.

1. Meaning Clues
    a. expectancy clues
    b. picture clues
    c. context clues

2. Visual Analysis
    a. configuration
    b. striking characteristics

3. Structural Analysis
    a. variants
    b. compounds
    c. derivatives

4. Phonics
    a. phonemic awareness
    b. initial single consonants
    c. medial consonants
    d. final consonants
    e. short vowels

f. long vowels and vowel combinations
   g. consonant combinations, two- and three-letter blends and digraphs
   h. r-controlled vowels
   i. syllabication
   j. auditory blending

During the Guided Reading Lesson, students are taught word recognition skills and then are given time to practice them.

Developing word recognition is a vital part of any reading program. In order to be a good reader, a student must have a storehouse of sight words, and he must be able to use all of the word recognition skills. He must be able to use them automatically, trying one technique that appears appropriate for an unknown word and quickly selecting another technique if the results are not satisfactory.

Emergent readers will come to words they do not know. In order to be accelerated in their reading, they must be able to choose the correct word analysis skill for the unknown word. No student can become a good reader if he is not able to integrate and use all of the word analysis skills.

Many times at-risk readers are given extensive practice in one skill to the exclusion of the others. When asked what they do when they come to words they do not know, students who are disabled in their reading often respond in one of two ways. The first response is that they ask someone, either a fellow classmate or their teacher. Perhaps they have been instructed by well meaning people that, when they come to words they do not know, they should just ask someone. Quite clearly, if emergent readers rely on the strategy of asking someone to tell them unknown words, they will never become independent readers.

The other common response that disabled readers often give when asked what they do when they come to words they do not know is to answer, "I sound it out." What the disabled reader means when he says he "sounds it out" is that he says the individual sound for every letter.

Roy is a classic example of an emergent reader whose strategy in decoding unknown words was to "sound it out." Roy was at the beginning of second grade, but because he had been retained in the first grade, he was actually in his fourth year of school. When I asked him what he did when he came to a word he did not know, he replied, "I sound it out." I gave him an emergent reader that had good, supportive picture cues, a book in which the pictures supported the print. I took

Roy through several pre-reading activities. We talked about the book, and then I asked Roy to set about the task of reading the print.

The first sentence on the page was, "The elephant has a red box." Roy did not know the word *the*. After he tried unsuccessfully to sound it out, I told him the word *the*. Then he went to the word *elephant*, and he meticulously said the sound for every letter in the word *elephant*. I said, "Roy, you really know what you do when you come to words you don't know. You do sound them out, don't you?"

Instead of learning to sound out words, Roy should have been taught to say, "Do I know a word that looks like that word and sounds like that word and would make sense here?" When at-risk readers only have one strategy or they have been taught and have subsequently practiced only one word recognition skill, teachers are prevented from accelerating them or moving them forward.

From the initial stages of Early Detection Necessary Action, students are taught all of the word recognition skills with equal importance being placed on each of them, and then the students are given time to practice and integrate those skills. Many new reading programs designed for at-risk readers are built around only one of the word recognition skills. Some computer programs just teach structural analysis activities. Video and audio reading programs often concentrate only on having students sit and listen to the phonetic pronunciation of words. Such was the case with Roy.

Roy's parents were concerned because Roy was not becoming a reader. To their great credit, they were eager to take any steps necessary to help him. When they saw an advertisement on TV about a reading program, they paid several hundred dollars to purchase the program. They then hired a high school student to make sure Roy spent an hour a day during the school year and two hours a day in the summer to go completely through the program. In their desperation and determination to help Roy, they were swayed by the enticing advertising that went along with this particular reading program. Often times, these reading programs are so difficult that both students and parents quickly abandon the effort and, in addition to the parent's financial loss, the child has gained nothing in his attempt to learn to read.

In Roy's case, though, a high school student was hired to make sure Roy performed all of the activities, and, indeed, Roy went completely through the program. But because this particular phonics program only emphasized the sounds of letters within words, Roy learned to sound out every letter in a word, and he believed he was reading. He thought the way to read was to simply look at the word and say the individual sound in every word. Roy developed a disabling practice and before he could make progress in reading, time had to be spent reprogramming his thinking about reading.

In Early Detection Necessary Action, students are instructed in and then given practice at using all of the word recognition skills which are taught during the word analysis portion of the Guided Reading Lesson. It is important to remember that students must be taught word recognition skills appropriate for their reading level. Reading is a sequential skill. Students gain confidence in word recognition skills and in their reading abilities at one level and then, using books with a gradient of difficulty, they move to the next level.

Early Detection Necessary Action students are taught the Guided Reading Lesson using books that are at the student's instructional level. The word recognition skill is always taken from the book the students will be reading, and after the skill is taught, the students immediately use the skill in the reading of a real book and in a writing activity.

Students receive practice using their previously taught word recognition skills by reading real books. Every day students review and reread books that have already been taught to them. There is also an independent reading time where students practice and read previously taught books or those that are at their independent reading level. It is imperative for teachers and students to understand that the student must do the work of reading and that the only way to become competent with word recognition is to practice using those skills reading real books.

The student must be taught the skills directly by his teacher and then he must practice under her careful, watchful guidance. Practice activities may be provided to the student throughout the day under the direction of the teacher or instructional aide or a parent volunteer in learning centers or with magnetic letters, computer programs, teacher-made games, commercial games and the like. While these are all acceptable aids to reinforce the teaching of word recognition skills, the primary practice must always come from the reading of real books. If there is only time to do one of the activities listed above, then eliminate the practicing of word recognition skills in isolation, and make sure time is provided for the student to read real books.

Early Detection Necessary Action students are taught word recognition skills and are then given time to practice each skill under the teacher's direction. The teacher uses activities that incorporate all three modalities to account for the various at-risk factors of the students in each group. If, for example, a student has trouble with auditory sequencing, he must receive good visual support to help him sequence the sounds. For a student with poor visual memory or inadequate visual configuration skills, the teacher must offer strong auditory instruction as well as an enhanced kinesthetic component.

The word recognition skills are taught using the Visual-Auditory Motor Method, the Word Family Method, the Kinesthetic Method, and the Phonics Method.

Visual-Auditory Motor Method

In the Visual-Auditory Motor Method, the teacher chooses words unfamiliar to the student, such as the sight words *yellow, what, where*. She presents each word and prints the word clearly on a white wipe-off board with a bright, contrasting color of ink.

"This is the word *yellow*. Take a good look at it. What is the word? Now make a sentence with the word. Close your eyes. Can you see the word with your eyes closed? Look again. What is the word? How many letters does it have? How many tall letters? What are the first three letters? What are the last three letters? Now close your eyes. Can you see the word with your eyes closed? Look again. What is the word? Take your finger and write the word on your arm. Write the first three letters. Now write the next three letters. What is this word?"

The teacher then removes the word and asks the student to write it. She instructs the student to compare his word with the one on the board. If it is incorrect, the teacher repeats the above procedure, presenting the word, pronouncing it, having him try to visualize it, and then asking him to write it again.

Sometimes it is necessary to show the word several times before the student is able to write it. If the student reproduces the word correctly, the teacher instructs him to write it again, covering up his previous writing to ensure he is recalling the word from memory rather than merely copying it. She checks each time to see that it is done correctly.

After a period of time has elapsed, she returns to the word for a review.

Word Family Method

When the student can grasp a visual procedure readily and shows some knowledge of letter sounds, the Word Family Method is integrated with the Visual-Auditory Motor Method. This technique of word analysis is especially useful for students who possess only rudimentary blending abilities and who are not yet able to copy with a letter-by-letter sound-blending procedure described under the Phonics Method. It affords a limited degree of independence in word analysis.

For example, a known word such as *man* may be transformed into *fan* or *can* by changing the initial consonant. After the student is able to use initial consonant replacement with word families, the teacher instructs him in final consonant replacement. "Can you take *man* and make it say *map*? Can you take *map* and make it say *mat*?"

Kinesthetic Method

The first time the *Kinesthetic Method* is used, the teacher presents a short orientation, describing and demonstrating the procedure and assuring the student that this method has helped other students become good readers. She writes a word with a crayon on paper in large script or print. The letters should be approximately two inches high. The student then traces the word with his finger, saying each part of the word as he traces it. The student repeats the process as many times as is necessary for him to write the word without looking at the original one.

When the student appears to know the word, he writes it on another sheet of paper. In case of errors or if the student hesitates and seems unable to complete the word, he retraces the entire word. He is not permitted to erase in order to correct errors. If he has difficulty recalling the word, he is encouraged to trace it over and over and then to write it without consulting the original writing.

Phonics Method

If a student shows the ability to blend three sounds that are presented orally, such as *b-a-t*, it is safe to try the Phonics Method. The teacher teaches or reviews the sounds of about four consonants and the short vowel *a*. The sounds of the letters are presented singularly as follows:

The teacher shows the student the lower case letter *m*: "This is *m* and the sound is *m*, as in *man*. Now I am going to give you some other words that begin with *m*. Listen and try to hear the *m* at the beginning of each word: m*eat*, m*ust*, m*ake*, m*ilk*. Can you hear the *m*? Now give me some words." The teacher helps with suggestions, if necessary.

Teaching the short vowel sound of *a*: "This is *a* and the sound is *a*, as in *apple*. Now I am going to say a word quickly, then slowly. Listen. The word is *c-a-t*. Now I am going to say it slowly: *c-a-t*. This is how it looks in writing. See if you can put the letters together to make *cat*." She then asks the student to sound out the word, helping him if necessary. She proceeds by showing the student how he can change the word to *mat, fat, sat*.

The teacher then writes a sentence containing the words: *The fat cat sat on the mat*. She changes the final sounds: *sat* to *sad*; *mat* to *man*; *fat* to *fan*. She dictates the words to ascertain whether the student can write them and sound them out as he writes them. She presents words in mixed order: *sat, fan, mad, bat*. If the student is able to read them, there is evidence he is likely to succeed with a phonics approach.

If a student shows lack of blending ability or is unable to name words that begin with sounds, it is advisable to postpone the use of the phonics procedure until after he has had training in phonemic awareness, auditory discrimination and sound blending. The student who has not developed a phonemic awareness has a poor auditory memory or auditory sequencing problems and cannot become a good reader using a program that emphasizes the phonics method.

<u>Combining Methods</u>

Combining the Word Family Method with the Visual-Auditory Motor Method and the Kinesthetic Method helps the student use his strong modality to support his weak modality. This combination of methods is used as a starting point to ensure success in learning to read from the initial stages of reading instruction. Before long, such procedures must be supplemented by other methods because a successful reader must have a variety of techniques at his command. Once the student has gained enough understanding of the sound-symbol correspondence, he can profit from the phonics method.

In Early Detection Necessary Action groups, the teacher is seated at a table with the students facing her. This enables the students who are having auditory difficulties to see the movement of the teacher's mouth as she forms, pronounces and repeats words and gives her the opportunity to make sure the students, particularly those with visual problems, are attending to the lesson. It is also important for the teacher to be at the same level as the students and to be able to touch all of the students who are in the group.

In taking special care to make sure that students receive instruction in all of the word recognition skills, Early Detection Necessary Action teachers must keep a chart and make sure all of the word recognition skills are receiving equal amounts of attention. This visual reminder prevents the chance that the student is relying on and becoming more practiced in one of the word recognition skills to the exclusion of the others.

The structure, then, of Early Detection Necessary Action is to teach students at their instructional level; to teach word recognition skills which are taken from the book they are preparing to read; to give the students an opportunity to practice word recognition skills; and to put the newly taught skills into printed form. The teacher is seated at a table with the students at their level where she can see them and touch them; the lessons are taught in a small group; and as the students are practicing the word recognition skills, the activities require them to use all three modalities.

Categories of Word Recognition Skills

There are four major categories of word recognition skills. First, meaning is used as a cue to decode an unknown word. Next is visual analysis, followed by structural analysis, and finally, phonetic analysis. Often, meaning is used as the expectant cue or picture cue and the word is just expected to be there, but the phonetic cues and visual cues must be utilized to see if the meaning word is correct for that configuration. For example, when reading the passage, "The bunny is white," the student just expects the word *bunny* to be there, but he has to use his visual and phonetic skills to make sure that it is the word *bunny* instead of the word *rabbit* or the word *hare*. So it is impossible to separate these skills and say that they can be used in isolation.

Using Meaning As a Cue

In order to be a good reader and to make progress, all of the word recognition skills must be used. During the portion of the Guided Reading Lesson that deals with vocabulary development and the pre-reading activities, the student learns to use meaning as his cue. In the story, *The Baby Gets Dressed*, for example, the teacher explains to the students that the story is about a baby and all the different things the baby puts on when she gets dressed.

The teacher asks the students to list some of the things a baby puts on when she gets dressed. As the students respond, she lists those things on a board. She then says to the students, "Let me read all of these things the baby may put on when she gets dressed," and the teacher puts her hand under each word as she reads: *pants, shirt, socks, shoes, dress.* If there are words in the book the students have not mentioned, the teacher makes sure she tells them so they will expect those words in the story. Such instruction is that part of the Guided Reading Lesson known as *Tell Them Everything They Need To Know.*

In this particular story, the baby puts on a petticoat. Children in today's society are not familiar with the word *petticoat*, so the new vocabulary word for that day would be *petticoat*. The teacher introduces the students to the new word before they read the book as preparation for them to anticipate and guess and use meaning to decode. She understands that the students cannot use meaning to decode the word *petticoat* if they do not know the word *petticoat* and what it means, so she may say, "In this story today, there is a fancy new word that we are going to learn and it means the same thing as slip. When I was a little girl, we always wore petticoats under our dresses." If the teacher is wearing a slip, she may show the students the edge of the slip and say, "This is what we call a slip today, but when I was a little girl, it was called a petticoat. Now everyone say *petticoat* and let me write this word down. I bet this word is going to be in the story. Do you think you will know this word when we come to it? Now let's read these vocabulary words again." She puts her hand under each word and reads the words with the students. The students use meaning to decode these words, matching them with the visual, structural, and phonetic configuration of the words.

The teacher has built the expectation and given them a base. During the vocabulary-building portion of the lesson the students are provided with all of the meaning vocabulary for that story. The three major types of meaning cues are expectancy, picture, and context.

Meaning Cues: Expectancy

Expectancy cues are related to a given topic. When students think about a general, topical concept, they get a psychological set for that topic. Certain ideas, especially words, come to the threshold of their consciousness, and they are ready to use them. When students discover, for instance, that they are going to be reading a story entitled *Bear's Breakfast*, the title itself causes them to expect certain words to be in the story. As they are reading, they take their expectancy, analyze the word, and match it with the other word recognition cues to help them eliminate possible words that could have the same meaning but would not have a graphemic fit.

Meaning Cues: Picture

Picture cues are equally important, and students should be encouraged to use them. Picture cues help build the concept of the story and often serve as the context cue in the early stages. Students take the picture cue and match it to the print on the page, though it must be a correct graphemic match. If a student is reading and comes to the word *mittens* and calls it *gloves*, then he would have used meaning but would not have matched it with the graphemic cues. In such a case, the teacher would use the beginning sound, match it to a word that would make sense, and ask the student to think of a word that begins the way that particular word begins.

Meaning Cues: Context

In the use of context cues, the surrounding words help determine unknown words. This is an important and effective strategy. In Early Detection Necessary Action, students must understand that they can decode an unknown word easily if they read the entire sentence and then ask themselves what word would make sense in the sentence. As the students are reading and come to words that are difficult, they must be asked to reread the sentence and guess what word would make sense.

Students who come from poor backgrounds of experience or students who have any type of auditory interference will have difficulty using meaning as a cue. Consequently, it is vital during the discussion of the story for the teacher to make sure she tells the students everything they need to know about the story so they can anticipate and guess and expect what words would be there.

Visual Analysis As a Cue

Visual analysis is the next word recognition skill. For students with visual memory problems, visual configuration problems, attending problems, or those who experience even the slightest visual interference, learning to use visual analysis is extremely difficult. Teachers must make sure they are reinforcing the students' ability to use visual analysis as a cue to help them in their reading. During word identification practice, students are taken through a detailed, visualizing approach to analyzing and remembering words. As the students are becoming competent at their visual analysis of the word, it is important for the teacher to show them the similarities and differences of words. Students who have visual problems do not automatically say, "How does that word start and how does it end and how is the word *what* different from the word *when* and the word *when* is like the word *then* except they are alike at their end but they are different at their beginning." Students who have any type of interference with their vision will not do those things automatically.

<u>Increasing Sight Word Recognition Through Visual Memory Activities</u>

From the beginning, students must be given practice attending to print in a specific, non-flexible way. One of the approaches is called "Increasing Sight Word Recognition Through Visual Memory Activities." Consider the word *barn*. The teacher says to the students, "We are going to learn the word *barn* today. This is the word *barn*. Look at the word *barn*. Tell me something about how it looks. How many letters does it have? What is the first letter? How many tall letters does it have? How many short letters does it have? Close your eyes. Can you see the word *barn* in your mind? What is its tall letter? Can you write the tall letter?"

The teacher gives the students twenty repetitions of the word *barn* where they have to actually visualize the word and see it in their memory and then put it on paper. This careful attention to having them recall, visualize and see a word in their minds not only helps them remember the specific word, but it helps them begin to do this on their own.

Students who need to become accelerated in their reading and have difficulty in their visual analysis abilities, find the *wh* words, the *th* words, and the little words that have no meaning to be stumbling blocks. When students come to the *wh* words, they simply have no idea how to go about decoding them. As part of their visual memory activities, the teacher must make sure the students are acquainted with the *wh* words. She must point out how they look, their similarities and differences, and whether or not they have the same two beginning letters. For at-risk students who have visual analysis problems, the teacher must help them develop a habit of careful visual inspection of problem words.

The same technique used in the teaching of individual words is also used in the teaching of the alphabet. Often students become confused with the tall letters. They will lump the *l, t, i, j,* and *f* together; the *b, d, t,* and *q*; or the *o, e,* and *c*. Because the letters are so similar, it is hard for students who have visual interference to remember the slight variances in these letters, and so they just lump them all together.

A similar approach as the visualizing memory activity is used for the teaching of the visual configuration of the letter. For example, list the *l, t, f,* and *j,* and talk about how they are all alike. The students must pay attention to how they are different. A *t* and an *f* have a cross, but an *f* has a curve at its top and a *t* does not. As students with visual problems are learning the alphabet, it is necessary to do these detailed techniques with them so they do not become sloppy about their visual attentiveness to print.

During oral reading, visual analysis helps the student understand that words in the written language are not flexible. As he learns a word, he must be made to understand that the word will always be the same, it will never change. Early on, students begin to have a lazy approach in their attention to print and are prevented from being accelerated in their reading. Jason is a classic example. With no signs hooked up with symbols, no knowledge of the reading process, it was no wonder that he, even in the sixth grade, could not identify the letter *a*. He was so confused in his knowledge and in his understanding and his concept about reading that after teaching him the word *and*, he continued to write *dna*. Jason was convinced this was the word *and*. He simply did not understand that words are static and that once he learned a word, the letters could not be moved around. Jason's problems were major, but for students with just the slightest confusion, moving forward in their reading is impossible.

Teaching students to use good visual analysis, teaching them the visual configurations of the word, and giving them the support and help they need is the only way for at-risk students to understand that words remain the same. They need to be taught that, once they learn a word, it will always be that word.

Students must also be taught to look at the beginning of the word, for it is at a word's beginning that the first cue is found. At-risk students do not understand that they need to look at the beginning of a word for information about decoding it. Instead, they might look at the middle or the end of the word. Therefore, students should become competent at looking at the beginning sound during the visual analysis portion of the lesson.

Structural Analysis As a Cue

While visual analysis of a word is extremely important and is a skill that readers must develop, being able to visually analyze the word does not help a student take what he knows about one word and generalize it to other words. That skill is known as structural analysis, and it is the skill that gives students the ability to recognize and decode hundreds of unknown words. Early Detection Necessary Action students are taught a spelling pattern or word family, and from that one pattern they are able to generalize and transfer the knowledge to other words in the same pattern.

Structural Analysis: Word Families

For example, the teacher presents *a n* and say to the students, "This *a n* at the end of a word says *an*. Let's all say that: *an*. Now if *a n* at the end of the word says *an*, I could put an *m* in front of it and make it say *man*." The teacher writes the *m*, and then the students read the word *man*. "Now how would I make the word say *tan*? What would I have to have at its end? What two letters make up that sound at the end of tan? Now what would I put in front of it to make it say *tan*? A *t*. If this is *man* and this is *tan*, how do I make it say *fan*?" And the teacher writes the word *fan*, and she goes through all of the words in that word family, letting the students supply the word to her whenever possible.

After the teacher lists all the words, the students read them as a group with the teacher. Then the teacher takes away her sample and has each student write *a n* at the top of their wipe-off boards. She directs the students, "See if you can make your word say *tan*. Let's see if you can make it say *man*. Let's see if you can make it say *ran* and *fan*. Now let's all read these words together: *man* and *fan* and *ran* and *tan*." It is important that the students pronounce the words with the teacher. After every word is generated, the teacher directs the students to wipe the boards clean and each student then comes up with some words of his own from that word family.

The teacher goes from student to student making sure they are staying on task, giving them cues to help them whenever necessary. It is vital to always watch over the students to eliminate any confusion and wrong assumptions about the sound that goes with the symbol or the word. For instance, if a student writes the word *fan* and says he has written *tan*, the teacher responds, "Well I know why you think that is the word *tan* because how does *tan* start...like *tom*, *tough* and *tell*? Now look at that. Is that a *t*? Does a *t* have a curve at its top? If that word is *tan* you need to fix it so that it begins with a *t*."

This type of careful watching over the student will help him remember the slight variances in the visual configurations of the letters as well as aid him in building his sight words. Begin with the *cvc* pattern words: the *at, ot, it,* and from there, go to the *cvc* plus *e*. After the students have learned the words and the word families, it is easier to teach them the phonetic rules. A list of spelling patterns is provided, but avoid choosing words from a list of phonemic spelling patterns. Look instead for words that have the phonemic spelling patterns in the book the students are going to read. If the student is reading the Wright Group book, *Dan, Dan the Flying Man,* for example, pull an *an* word out and teach that phonemic spelling pattern.

Teaching students to generalize about words that are in the same family or have a similar phonemic spelling pattern helps them build their sight words. In addition, it helps them transfer what they know about one word to other words with the same segment. As the students are learning the beginning *cvc* pattern words, they should begin to build up the ability to quickly recognize the beginning consonant sound by the use of initial consonant substitution.

If there are blends that appear in the word families, teach the blends, as well. For example, the students have been taught a phonemic spelling pattern and have learned the *op* family using the word *stop* as part of that family. The next day during the word recognition skill practice, teach the *st* blend, as in *stop*, asking, "What are other words that have *st* at their beginning?" The student then begins to gain skill and practice at double blends.

Structural Analysis: Compound Words

As compound words begin to appear in a student's reading, teach him to break the one big word into two small words. Do not expect the student to look for the small word within the big word. Direct him to take the compound word and break it into the two words that make up the one word. As early as the compound words begin to appear in reading, take the compound words out of their reading and say, "This is the word *in*; this is the word *to*. Those two words make the compound word, *into*. This is the word *to*; this is the word *day*. These two words together make up the one word, *today*. This is the word *out*; this is the word *side*. These two words when put together make the word, *outside.*" Visually begin helping the student recognize and become more familiar with the words that are compounds.

Structural Analysis: Variant Endings

Likewise, it is important that students pay attention to the endings of words. When they are reading, they must pronounce the variant forms of endings of words. As early as these forms begin to appear in their reading, take them from the book and work with them on that skill. In the books *I Like Playing, I Like Reading, I Like Running,* call attention to the fact that *i n g* at the end of the word says *ing* and that if *ing* is added to the word *walk*, it becomes *walking. Ing* added to *play* makes the word say *playing*. It is important that students start paying attention to these variant forms as soon as they appear. Many at-risk readers will leave off the endings of words, so they must be given good visual help and a thorough explanation of the endings. As always, the teacher must then provide them with the opportunity to practice. She must make sure that in their reading and in their writing, they are using the endings to the words.

Early on, students need to learn the different structures of what can be added to a root word. In the initial stages of reading, students who do not pay visual attention or who have auditory difficulties will disregard endings such as *s, ing, es*. During structural analysis, it is especially important for at-risk readers to pay careful attention to the endings of words.

A first step is to teach the added endings in words as they appear in the student's reading. If the text reads, "I like jumping," "I like running," "I like reading," "I like playing," each of the words is isolated by the teacher who writes the word *jump*, then the word *jumping*; the word *run*, then the word *running*; and so on in order to show the students the differences. She then instructs the students to say, *"jump, jumping; run, running."* The teacher then removes her sample and has the students write the word *jump*, and then adds *ing* at its end to make it say *jumping*. The teacher gives the students the visual for the root word and has them add the inflected ending.

On another day, the teacher presents the word in all of its forms: *jumps, jumped, jumping* and the students are instructed to read them together. She pulls other words from that day's book, and says, "Now make the word *walk* say *walks*," and the students write the word *walks*. "Now make the word *walk* say *walked*," proceeding in that manner. When the students are reading and they read the sentence, "The boy jump over the box," the teacher says to the students, "Let's go back and put our finger under that word. Look at its end. What does it have? What sound does it make when those two letters are at the end of a word? Let's go back and read that again. The boy..." and the students say, "*jumped*."

The teacher must make sure that the students are getting good, clear visual and auditory cues during their word analysis portion of the lesson and that when they are reading, they are paying attention to the print and reading exactly what is there. Print is not flexible, and the word *jumps* is not the word *jump*. When an element is added to a word, the word changes, and each of these elements carries a good deal of meaning. When students get sloppy and do not pay attention to all of the print, they are not able to use meaning or structure of language in print as cues.

The word *boy* with the letter *s* added now means more than one boy. The addition of *ed* to the word *jump* means that it happened in the past, so it changes the meaning of the sentence. When students are reading, it is important that they read and pay attention to the inflected forms of words.

<u>Structural Analysis: Contractions</u>

As soon as contractions begin to appear in the material the students are reading, the contracted form of the word is taken from the book and presented to the students. The teacher writes the word *don't* and makes a sentence: "I *don't* want to ride the bus home today." Then she makes a sentence with the two words, "I *do not* want to ride the bus home today." The word *don't* means the same as the two words *do not*.

The students make an oral sentence where they substitute the contraction for the two words that make up the contraction. Then the teacher writes the contracted form of the word and under it writes the two words. The students then analyze it visually to see what is different about the contracted form compared to the two words. The teacher gives the students three or four contractions and lets them see how the contraction is formed. She then takes the visual image away and writes the word *do not* and asks them to write the word *don't*. She might write the words *is not*, for example, and ask the students to write the word *isn't*. Such an exercise aids the teacher in assessing the student's visual recognition of the word and his understanding of how the word is formed.

When at-risk readers are reading and come to an unfamiliar contracted form of the word, it interrupts them. As soon as contractions begin appearing in reading, it is important to begin working on them during the word analysis portion of the Guided Reading Lesson. Contractions are easier to teach than other word analysis skills if the contracted form of the word is in the student's oral language. If the student does not have the contracted form of the word in his language, it is much more difficult to have him be able to read it in the printed form. Auditory children are especially confined in their knowledge of contractions.

Phonetic Analysis

Word identification skills are separated by grade. Initial consonants are taught first, and as children develop the phonemic awareness of print, they become better able to hear the individual sounds in words. With the acquisition of this skill, students then are able to match up the sound in the word with the visual configuration of the letter associated with that sound.

As students become competent with phonemic awareness, they also should be learning the visual configurations of the alphabet letters and the sound associated with each letter. Along with sound/symbol correspondence, they are taught key words. For instance, in teaching the letter *h*, the teacher associates the letter with the sound of *horse* and *house* and *home*. She writes those words in a list, pointing out to the students how they begin. After reading the words aloud with the teacher, the students suggest other words that have the same beginning sound.

The teacher has the students describe a lower case *h* as a letter with a tall stick and a hump. Similarly, she discusses the differences between a lower case *h* and an upper case *H*, explaining how they are different. The students are provided with different types of practice activities to help them become competent with describing letters. Such activities take place during the learning center time.

In kindergarten, careful attention should be given to make sure that the students are developing a good, visual identification of the letter, that they can link a sound with the letter, have a key word associated with it, and can use it in their writing. Once students get to the first grade, teachers no longer have the luxury of working only on the alphabet. At the beginning of first grade, identify the letters the student knows and letters he does not know and then work with the unknown letters during the time he is being taught to read.

Word identification skills are taught at different times, and it is not necessary to start at the top and work to the bottom. One day you may work on a blend and the next day you may work on a contraction and the following day you may work on a spelling pattern. Pull the word recognition skill that is at the level of print in the current book. The goal is that by the time the student is reading at the first grade level, he is also competent with all of these word recognition skills.

In Early Detection Necessary Action groups, a chart is maintained to ensure that each student is gaining knowledge of and practice with all of the word recognition skills. For example, on Monday the teacher may work on the *an* family because the students have read *Dan, Dan the Flying Man*. At the same time, instruction is provided on the beginning sounds and the teacher would note such instruction on the chart. On Tuesday, the students are introduced to an *ing* ending, and a similar notation is made. On Wednesday, instruction is given on the function words, the *wh* words, the *th* words, and *a*. The following day, a consonant blend is taught, and on Friday, an auditory blending activity. Each day's instruction is recorded on the chart.

A carefully detailed chart allows the teacher to monitor the word recognition skills that are being taught and enables her to judge how much time she is spending teaching reading compared to the time the students are actually practicing the word recognition skills in the act of reading.

Chapter Seven

Write Every Day

Writing — breaking the code, mastering the graphemic system, understanding the alphabetic principles — is critical if a student is to become a good reader. Students must master the coding system and be able to use it automatically. Three cueing systems are used in reading: the graphemic — sound and letter patterns; the syntactic — sentence patterns; and the semantic — meaning. Of the three, the graphemic coding system is unique to the written language.

Attending to the many elements of the code is required in order to read and write. It is a tedious, specific, non-flexible task and one which occurs only during the act of reading and writing. Because print is rigid, good readers must have a perfect, practiced, fluent understanding of the slightest variance in the details of print. Even the least misconception keeps the student from making progress. Eventually, those misconceptions, however minor they might seem, build and become impenetrable barriers. The task of reading and writing with fluency then becomes impossible, causing frustration and a negative emotional reaction to reading and to school.

For students who have one or more of the at-risk factors, learning the numerous, detailed, specific elements of the code is extremely difficult. Students with visual interference do not attend to the slight differences in the letter formation and visual configuration of similar words. They get the wrong idea about where print begins on the page, what the spaces between the words mean, and where a word begins. Clearly, these students develop numerous disabling practices when dealing with print.

If, for example, a student with visual interference is asked to write the word *jump*, his tactic might be to look across the top of the board at the ABC chart, saying the alphabet in order until he comes to the letter *j*, which he then writes. The student understands beginning sounds, so he knows the *j* makes the beginning sound of the word *jump*. What he is unable to remember is the visual configuration of the letter. The coping tactic this student employs in his writing alerts his teacher to the problem, which she can then proceed to correct.

Children with various types of visual interference match similar letters together. Eventually the *c, e, a,* and *o* begin to look alike in their writing, as do the tall letters l, t, f, k, and h. Lumping similar letters together rather than remembering the slight, individual variances becomes much easier for these students. They fail to notice the differences in the *f* and the *t*, for instance.

Unlike their lower case counterparts, many upper case letters — such as the *B* and *D* — are more distinctive, making them easier to remember. Consequently, students often use capital letters in their writing, eliminating the need to remember the details of forming lower case letters. Knowing which side of the stick the circle is placed in the lower case *b* or *d* is far more difficult than recalling the look of the upper case *B* or *D*. Be assured that if a student is inappropriately using capital letters in his writing, he does not have a good, clear understanding of letters in his reading.

Students who have auditory interference have difficulty matching the sound to the corresponding symbol. Hearing and sequencing sounds in words is extremely hard work for these students. Often they hear only the last sound in a pronounced word. In the word *mother,* for instance, they hear only the *r*, and it is that letter they use as they begin to write *mother*. Students with auditory interference often memorize sight words and can effectively control their writing to match those few sight words. Again, this is a coping mechanism to help the student deal with the difficult task of writing.

Other tactics employed by the at-risk student include relying on someone to tell them how to spell the word, or copying a word list from the board or picture dictionary. They become adept at avoiding the difficult task of matching the sounds with the visual configurations. While students with visual interference are able to identify and make the beginning sound in a word, they are not able to match up the visual configuration of the letter.

Students with auditory interference can write the letter and identify the letter name, but they cannot match the sound with it, and in their writing, they cannot match the sounds in the sequencing of the words. These students can name the letters, but they cannot say a word that begins with the letter.

Students who come from deprived backgrounds, who have no experience with written language, may not make the connection between spoken language and written language. These students have no concept of books, stories, letters, words, or sentences. They do not understand that print — which to them is nothing more than squiggles on a page — carries the message. They have no comprehension that those squiggles represent talk on a page. These students are not familiar with the structure of language the way it appears in print.

It is an erroneous notion to assume that a child can learn to read if he can learn to talk. This theory does not take into consideration the complex differences between talking and reading. Mastering the coding system — understanding the orthographic and the graphemic components in that system — is a specific, non-flexible, tedious task. This fact must never be underestimated.

For students with one or more of the at-risk factors, mastering the coding system is full of land mines. They do not understand what letters, words, and sentences are. They look at a word at the end or middle, not the beginning. They do not comprehend that the spaces between words signal the beginning of a new word. They lump visually similar letters together. They link the wrong sound with the wrong visual symbol. They cannot sequence the sound with the word. They go about decoding using an improper motion. Misconceptions that are repeatedly practiced ultimately become ingrained in the reading and writing of at-risk students.

If a student writes using random letters, then he knows that letters somehow make words, but he does not understand that there is a sound-symbol match and that a word is static. He does not understand that the word *is* will always be *is* and that the letter *i* comes before the letter *s*. If he succeeds in writing the correct beginning letter, then he is competent with the sound-symbol correspondence in its initial position. If he leaves spaces, writes to the right margin of the page and returns to the left, then his directionality is on target. A student's writing reflects his reading abilities.

Do not fail to understand what hard work it is for at-risk students to match sounds with symbols and then transfer that knowledge to paper. Observe each student carefully, guiding him to stop, think, and say the word. Teach him to hear the beginning sound, and alert him to listen for the next sound. If there is a word the student should know from sight, help him remember it. Coach the student to leave spaces between words.

The *Write Every Day* portion of the Guided Reading Lesson provides an unparalleled opportunity for the teacher to work one on one with the student, focusing heavily on the sound-symbol connection. The teacher draws from the child whatever the child knows and models what is unknown, reinforcing and guiding approximations along the way: "What did you want to write? Mother? Say that word. What do you hear at its beginning? Good! Put that down. Say it again. Do you hear anything else? Put that down."

On the average, the teacher should spend two to three minutes with the student, guiding him through his writing activity, which can be as simple as a single sentence. While the teacher serves as the coach, she must not do the writing for the student; rather, she must help the student take what he knows about reading, visualize it in his head, and transfer his understanding to print. When the student begins to realize a measure of success, the teacher's involvement can diminish somewhat. Be aware that even the slightest success can take much longer than what is typical in other students.

White wipe-off boards and dry erase markers are used in the writing exercises. The markers are bright, give a good visual representation, and are easy to manipulate. After each session, the boards are erased so there are no errors remaining to haunt the at-risk student.

Writing follows predictable stages. In the beginning, students believe that a picture tells the message, so they draw squiggles which they presume tell the story, a normal and developmentally appropriate belief in kindergartners. Then they begin to realize that signs carry a message. An obvious example is McDonald's familiar golden arch, which a child might "read" to mean French fries and hamburgers. Next they begin to write random letters, paying no attention to the sound-symbol correspondence. They begin using the initial letter to represent most words they want to write. Eventually, they begin to leave spaces. When their knowledge of sight words increases, they begin writing words using inventive spelling that reflects initial, medial and ending sounds, adding some vowels. The writing pattern continues until it becomes easy, and they can write effortlessly and with fluency.

Many students move quickly from one stage of writing to the next, but for the at-risk student, the task of matching sounds with symbols, visualizing them, and transferring them from their mind to print is such hard work they avoid the task. They get stuck in one stage and practice that stage, developing incorrect, disabling habits that become the way they believe print to be.

At-risk students must receive support, direct instruction and effective, repetitive, practice activities to move from one stage to the next. Without the careful, watchful guidance of the teacher, at-risk students will never understand that they must leave spaces between words, that there is a difference between words, that there is a difference between the tall letters. The writing time is the time to catch these misconceptions and help the student perfect and practice the right concepts about print.

Effective writing requires the student to do his own work in matching sounds and symbols to tell the message. Early Detection Necessary Action students do not copy during the writing period. Copying is a much easier task and does not teach the student to make the reading-writing link in his head. Many at-risk students can copy beautifully and have no idea what the copy represents.

Do not provide the students with a work book, or let them look words up in a picture dictionary. Do not let them look back in the book to find correct spellings. Avoid telling students the word or spelling it for them, even if they request help. Beginning with the first day of first grade, establish the boundaries for the written response during the guided lesson. Eliminate the tendency to draw a picture to tell their responses. Many at-risk students prefer to draw, and they will draw a picture, then proceed to give a long, detailed oral explanation about what the story tells. Every time a student is allowed to draw in order to convey a message, the belief that a picture carries the message is reinforced, and they have not practiced making the critical reading-writing links.

Direct the student to give a written response: "Today we read a book about school. The book talked about fun things to do at school. I would like for you to write me a story about what you like to do at school. Jeremy, what do you like? Scott, what do you like?" After hearing their verbal responses, the teacher says, "Write that for me."

If the student begins to draw a picture, say, "We aren't illustrating today. We are writing a story. You were going to write, 'I like ball.' Can you write the word *I*? Good. Now leave a space. *Like* is an *ike* word. What three letters make that sound at the end of a word? Great! Now say the word *like*. Do you know the letter that makes the *l* sound, just like in *lemon, less* and *late*? Great! Now leave a space. Say the word *ball*. What do you hear at the beginning? Good. Put that down. Say the word again. What do you hear? Put that down. Say the word again. Do you hear anything else? Okay, you did a great job!"

The student's written response to the sentence, *I like ball*, could look like this: *i lk BTL*. Then the teacher says to the student, "Look at the *B* in *ball*. Could you take the top circle off of the *B*? Good! Now that makes a lower case *b*." The white wipe-off boards enable the student to take his hand and make the adjustment to the letter. Remember that students use upper case letters as a crutch, and if they use them in their writing, be assured they do not know lower case letters in their reading. Knowledge of lower case letters in reading is imperative in saying beginning sounds.

In this particular example, the writing activity was structured to include those skills the students already had been taught. They previously had learned the word *like* as a sight word. The *ike* word family with initial consonant substitution, was taught during the word analysis part of the Guided Reading Lesson. For example, the students were asked to write the word *like* and consonant/vowel/consonant plus silent *e* variants such as *bike, hike, pike*. The sentence pattern and the background for the writing activity had been used in the phrase book the students had been taught and then read during the Guided Reading Lesson.

Many times when a student is asked to write about his favorite part, he replies, "I don't have a favorite part," or "I don't remember anything." These are typical responses for a student who seeks to avoid the frustrating, difficult task of writing. The teacher responds by saying, "That's okay. I have a favorite part. You may write about that. My favorite part is when the elephant falls in the river." And she would proceed to help the student write and match up sounds with symbols, coaching him in his task of writing. It is important to make sure the students spend the time set aside for writing and reading doing just that.

On some occasions, the writing activity may involve asking the students to write all of the *at* or *ot* word families, to write the color words or the number words, or to simply write all the words they know. The writing activities can follow the pattern book the students have been taught with the teacher providing the pattern to the students who, in turn, supply the meaning words.

The teacher may dictate a sentence to the students and help them go about the task of converting it from their head to paper. The sentence should be simple and have no more than forty phonemes: "I like to play ball. My mom will play ball with me. Help me find a good ball." The teacher might choose to have the students write a list of words that begin with *m*, or have them make a list of things they like or dislike.

The writing activity should take about five minutes at the end of the Guided Reading Lesson. Over the course of a week, the teacher takes time to help guide the students through their writing, giving them the help and support they need to be able to practice making the critical sound-symbol links. All along, the teacher is checking the students' writing against the educator's checklist, Monitoring Writing Progress provided at the end of this chapter.

The modeled writing process takes place during the time students are in the initial, emergent stages of learning to read and write. This occurs during the Cut-up Story. In the modeled writing, the teacher provides the opportunity for the students to go through the thought processes that occur in writing. Students collaborate with the teacher to bring the sounds and symbols together and to make decisions regarding the use of print conventions. Print, when it is created with the students, then becomes the material used to teach those same conventions in their reading.

The following is an example of modeled writing that would take place during the Cut-up Story activity: The teacher and students decide on a topic. As the students relate the sentence they want to contribute to the story, they are guided through the writing process. If the students are writing the sentence, *I like ham for breakfast*, the teacher may say, "Let me write the word *I*. How do we go about doing that? This is how we start. This is the word *I*. How many letters are in the word *I*? Now we need to write the word *like*. Let's leave a space. Who can tell me what letter we would need to use to make the sound we hear at the beginning of the word *like*? Okay, now this is how we make the letter *l*, like lemon, lesson, lake."

The teacher writes the word *like*, very carefully drawing the *l* as the children are watching, and then she elicits from them, *like*. *Ike* at the end of the word says *ike*, or she may say the word *like*. "What else do you hear?" and she writes the responses and says, "Well, we also have an *e* at the end." She mentions any other letters they have left out and writes those down. The process continues until the end of the sentence.

From the beginning of the Cut-up Stories, the teacher models the students' level of writing and helps elicit from them while she models. The modeling of writing for students is crucial and occurs during the Cut-up Story section of Early Detection Necessary Action training.

During the modeled writing, the teacher writes the correct responses given by the students, and she focuses on the letters and the letter/sound relationship by asking the questions that will lead the students to hear and make the visual and phonetic connections. After she finishes writing the sentence, she may say, "Let's go back and read this. 'I like ham.' How many words are there? How many letters are there in the word *like*? How many letters are in the word *ham*?" And she would continue this way until she finishes the Cut-up Story. After the Cut-up Story is written and the students have been guided through the process of getting the chart to the sentence strips, to the words, and then to each individual story, the students learn all those elements of print during the week the teacher is reviewing and working with the Cut-up Story.

Modeling the writing process occurs during the time the students are in readiness and are in the early pre-primer levels of reading. The teacher's modeling begins with the origination of a story idea. She then models the process of telling the story, coaching the students to tell the story in their own words. The teacher might choose to retell a familiar story with a different twist, perhaps using different adjectives or nouns, or the story can be an experience the students have all shared. Each student then is asked to contribute a section of the story. As the teacher actually converts the language to print, she wants to be specific about engaging the students in helping her come up with all the necessary elements of converting the spoken word to print. After the story is written, the students can make illustrations to match the print on the page.

In Early Detection Necessary Action groups, writing is the window to the way students go about seeing print. Writing allows the teacher to know exactly what the student is doing when he is reading, presenting her an important opportunity to recognize, understand, and rectify the student's misconceptions and to see how the student is developing in his coding abilities. During the exercise of writing, the student is making reading-writing links. He is taking what he knows visually about the code, matching it to the sound associated with the symbol, putting them all together, and then forming the visual representation on paper.

In the Guided Reading Lesson, students write daily, giving them the opportunity to use the skills they need to master in each stage of reading and providing practice in their coding abilities. The Write Every Day activity is not the type of writing used to relay any kind of message, nor is it meant to entertain, to give information, or to develop writing fluency. Such writing is part of any good language arts program in which Early Detection Necessary Action students participate as part of their regular class work. The Write Every Day activity is a tool used to identify and clear up misconceptions, essential if the student is to become a good reader.

Educator's Checklist
Monitoring Writing Progress

Student's Name _____ **School** _____

	Date	Date	Date	Observations
Writing is drawing.				
Writes symbols to represent letters				
Random letters				
Leaves spaces				
Initial consonants for whole words				
Correct directional movement				
Uses capitals as a crutch B E F L D I				
Correct sound symbol transfer of similar letter l f h i j c e				
Uses some sight words correctly				
Initial and final consonants for words				
Initial, final, medial consonants				
Uses vowels in correct places				
Writes one sentence				
Writes two sentences				
Uses a period and capital letter in correct place				
Writes three or more sentences				
Uses beginning blends				
Uses many sight words correctly				
Uses ending blends				
Selects topics				

	Date	Date	Date	Observations
Uses endings – ing, ed, ly, er				
Story has a beginning, middle, end				
Grammar				
. " " ' ? ! ,				
Uses contractions				
Writes a title				
Expresses a message				
Spells most sight words correctly				
Uses inventive spelling for rich vocabulary				
Examples:				
Uses spelling rules				
Examples:				
Adding				
Expanding				
Rearranging				
Deleting				
Checks spelling				
Punctuation				
Grammar				
Publishes in a variety of forms				

Chapter Eight

Cut-up Story

The purpose of the Cut-up Story exercise is to help emergent readers develop a crisp, clear, correct concept of print. Never assume that children share the adult perception of print. M.D. Vernon and others found that children who fail in reading share certain, common characteristics which are described as "...cognitive confusion" and the "lack of a system about the whole reading process."

When students are asked to work on print, they develop a system to accomplish the task. At-risk students develop incorrect notions about print and practice these misconceptions every time they look at print. They do not know that print is inflexible; rather, they think the arrangement of letters in words can change. They look at the end of the word for the beginning sound, just as Jesse did. And, like Jerome, some students do not know that the white spaces separate words, nor do they know how to follow a line of print. Many begin reading from the right of a line of print and proceed to the left; some read in a column down the page; others may skip around, picking up a word in random order.

Many students begin to develop these misconceptions about print early in kindergarten and then practice them for the remainder of their school careers. As students receive additional instruction in reading, they incorporate the new instruction into their misconceptions and become all the more confused.

Careful attention must be given to the students' development of a crisp, clear, correct concept of print, and then they must be given the opportunity to practice. Students cannot be accelerated in their reading abilities if they are not working on print in the correct way. The Cut-up Story process gives students practice looking at and manipulating print correctly. It is designed so that students cannot reconstruct the story using the wrong concept of print.

Cut-up Stories develop good reader concepts, teaching students the basics of print. They learn what a letter is, what a word is, what a sentence is. They learn word-to-word correspondence, spatial layout, tracking, directionality, return sweep, and how to use meaning and the beginning sound to decode an unknown word. They begin to understand that print carries the message of the story.

In preparing a Cut-up Story, the teacher determines the structure of the story. She controls the sight words and guides the students to supply the meaning words. Since the Cut-up Story is used to teach students to read, it should always be at the students' reading level.

At the beginning of kindergarten, the cut-up story is at the student's readiness level. In introducing the Cut-up Story as a learning activity, the story should follow the format of a caption book. For example, it should read: "The shirt." "The sock." "The shoe." The structure of the story changes as the students make gains in their reading abilities, and ultimately they will be reading, "The shirt is blue." "The shoe is green."

The topic of the Cut-up Story is determined from a variety of sources. The teacher may guide the students in selecting a topic that coordinates with other lessons such as social studies, science, health, and math, or that demonstrates a common or shared experience.

The teacher selects the sight words and the structure to match the group's reading abilities. She then guides the students in an oral discussion to elicit the meaning words for the story. The teacher reviews the sight word *a*, practices beginning consonants, and interjects the word families, *an* and *at*. She helps the students stay focused, as in this example:

> Teacher:
> "This morning, we read a story about a cat and all the things a cat likes to do. What are some things a cat likes to do?"
>
> Jeremy:
> "I had a cat, and it runs through the whole house. If a door is open, it runs outside."
>
> Teacher:
> "So, Jeremy, we could say, 'A cat can run.'"

Day One

On the first day of the Cut-up Story learning activity, the teacher gathers a small group of no more than six students. The process is much easier for the teacher, and the students get more practice if the group contains no more than six students.

The teacher elicits suggestions and guides the students in selecting a topic. The story is recorded by the teacher on a piece of chart paper. The students and the teacher create a title for the story. Then the teacher talks with each students and asks them to provide a sentence for the story. The teacher encourages the students to speak in complete sentences by modeling standard English and by rephrasing the student's sentence.

As the teacher is recording the story, she points out the conventions of print. She involves the students in the process of taking what is in their heads and converting it to the printed word. As she completes each sentence, the group reads the sentence to the teacher while she points to each word.

Once the story is written on the chart, each student, using a pointer, takes a turn reading the completed story which may look like this:

A Cat

A cat can run.

A cat can play.

A cat can jump.

A cat can scratch.

<u>Illustrations - Each Child, Each Page, Each Day</u>

Make a booklet for each child in the group using a separate page for each sentence. The students will illustrate one page daily. By the end of the week, the students have a completed book which is at their reading level and which they helped to write.

<u>Day Two</u>

The following day, write each sentence on a sentence strip. Copy the sentence exactly as it is on the chart, which is always visible to provide support. Give the students their sentence strip and have them take turns reading them aloud. After each student reads his sentence, he places the strip in the correct pocket, looking at the chart for assistance. The sentence strips should match the chart word for word, space by space.

After the students have placed their strips in the correct pocket, the teacher points to each word as the group reads the story. The teacher then removes the sentence strips and mixes them up like a puzzle. The students take turns matching the sentence strips to the chart and placing them in the pocket chart.

The students illustrate page two of their individual books.

Day Three

On the third day of the Cut-up Story learning activity, hand the students their sentence strips, and give them an opportunity to read their sentences. The students then cut the sentence strip into words while the teacher observes. Students place their words in a pocket chart to match the chart story. Students take turns reading the story. The teacher places the words out like a puzzle, and the students reconstruct the story. As the students reconstruct the story, they are forced to look at print in the correct way. In order to put the story together matching word to word, they must look at the beginning letter and use correct directionality.

Following this activity, the students illustrate page three in their books.

Day Four

On the fourth day, the teacher places the words like a puzzle, and each student reconstructs the story. As the students reconstruct the story, the group reads it together. By now, the students have seen the words numerous times throughout the week. The teacher guides them through a word analysis activity taken from the story. For this story, for example, she might teach the *at* and *an* word families.

The students illustrate page four in their books.

Day Five

The students read the story on the chart to begin day five of the Cut-up Story learning activity. For further reading practice, select another story from a former week, and let each student read that story.

By this point, the students' books should be complete. The teacher guides the students as they read from their books. Make sure the students have a word-to-word correspondence as they read. Give each student an opportunity to read the entire book. Encourage the students to take their books home to read to their parents, but remind them to return the books to school.

Keep the books displayed in a prominent place in the room. Use them frequently to review previous word recognition skills and to read during independent reading time.

The Cut-up Story learning activity is an invaluable tool in teaching emergent readers how to read. In addition to creating something from which students can learn to read and providing them with something they can read, the Cut-up Story builds site words and teaches beginning sounds. It insists that students focus on tracking and directionality. It aids them in acquiring oral language skills, and it develops and strengthens the innate rules of both language and print.

In imparting enthusiasm for reading, the Cut-up Story is unparalleled, for it provides students with both ownership and authorship, something which brings them gratification and pride.

Chapter Nine
Read Togethers

The Read Together learning activity gives young readers practice in a variety of skills essential to becoming good readers. Of major importance, the Read Together builds the innate sense of the structure of language as it appears in print. In addition, it is a learning activity which develops efficient eye movement, including tracking and directionality and the return sweep.

The Read Together gives students practice and reinforcement on concept-of-print skills: story title; story progression; word-to-word correspondence; the knowledge of what a letter, word, and sentence are; and the awareness that the print, not the picture, carries the message. Each successive time the student reads the story, he recalls the context of the story from the initial Read Together activity and uses his memory of the story and his graphemic knowledge to decode the words on the page. Finally, the modeling by the teacher and the repetitive readings by the student during the Read Together activity allows the emergent reader to read the story fluently in the author's voice using the proper phrasing and expression.

Good readers use meaning as the first cue to decode unknown words. As their eyes move across print, they automatically anticipate, predict and guess what word will be next. They use visual and sound cues to narrow the field of their prediction and then they double check their choice. In order to use meaning as a cue, students must be familiar with the structure of language as it appears in print. Reading to young children develops this innate sense of printed language. Good readers share the experience of having been read to in their early years. Children who have not been read to or those with auditory interference do not have this essential knowledge. The repetitive reading of books with a predictable story in a small group setting accelerates the student's ability to use the structure of print as a decoding cue.

The repetitive language in pattern books helps students develop familiarity with new vocabulary and with the structure of language, and it builds self-confidence in their ability to use the words correctly within the structure of language. Even at an early age, children are able to supply missing words to their favorite nursery rhymes after having heard them only a few times.

The rhythm and rhyme of Read Together books present cues that do not exist in spoken language. Knowing or being able to predict what comes next allows the student to be a risk-taker with language and ideas. The Read Together process helps students develop greater familiarity with the three cueing systems used in reading: syntax, sentence structure; semantics — the meaning in language; and graphemics — the relationship between sounds and letters.

Good readers focus on a point and, as their eyes move across print, they pick up visual and sound cues to check their prediction. Their eyes work as a team, sweeping back to the left margin of the page as they prepare to read the next line of print. If students have difficulty with focusing, with attending, or with eye teaming, concentrating on print is hard work. These students begin to avoid the process altogether or find short cuts to assist them through the lesson. Such practices become disabling.

Read Together activities are instrumental in developing efficient eye movement. As in any physical skill, repetition and practice make eye movement more natural for the student, eliminating the possibility of having the student develop his own method of compensating for his inability to see print correctly. Read Together activities aid greatly in lessening the chance that the student's eyes will jump randomly over the print, or that he will read to the center of a line then drop down to the next line, or that he will read from left to right and then read the next line from right to left.

Repetitive reading enables the student to read with fluency and proper phrasing. Students who are in the beginning stages of reading cannot read unfamiliar printed material with fluency. Their knowledge of print is so limited they are forced to stop and work on each word. The process of the Read Together activity allows students to read with proper phrasing and fluency as they use their memory of the story and their graphemic knowledge to decode the words.

Book Selection

There are specific criteria in choosing a Read Together book. The format of the book is important. There should be more than one line of print on most of the pages. The print should be large and bold and should be written in a straight line from left to right rather than presented in story bubbles or scattered on the page. The illustrations should carry the story line and support the print on the page. The length of the book should accommodate a forty-five minute lesson.

The book should be appropriate for young children. Neither the vocabulary nor the story line should be too advanced for first or second grade students. It should be a story that students enjoy hearing and reading numerous times.

The book should use rhyme, rhythm, alliteration, phoneme substitution, and repetition in the story line. The book should have a predictable pattern, repeating certain structures of language, words, phrases, or events. The book should present a complete story that is easy to remember.

Because the book is read repeatedly, it should be at or slightly above the student's frustration level. It is also extremely important that each student have a copy of the book. Equally important is the group setting. The students should be seated at a table where the book can be stabilized and easily controlled by the student. The teacher is seated facing the students so that she can observe and guide them.

Procedure - Day One

On the first day of the Read Together activity, the teacher introduces the story by inviting the students to talk about the front and back cover of the book as well as the title page. Based on that discussion, she then asks them to predict what the story is about. The teacher guides the students to look at the illustrations on each page and encourages them to tell her what the illustrations reveal about the characters, action and setting of the story. The teacher encourages them to activate their prior knowledge about experiences they may have had that could be related to the story.

At this stage in the Read Together activity, the teacher does not attempt to read the print and does not call attention to the print, though she may encourage the students to guess and talk about the words they may expect to find in print. She allows the students to enjoy the illustrations and express their opinions as they explore the book. The teacher should show enthusiasm in anticipation of reading the story.

Once the students are familiar with the book and are excited about hearing the story, the teacher reads it to the students. During the first reading, the students listen to the story. They do not have to follow along or read with the teacher. If a student wants to read, it is permissible.

After the first reading, the students are instructed to follow along. They are instructed to place a finger under each word as it is read. During the reading, the teacher observes the students, making sure they are pointing accurately. This is a difficult task for both the student and the teacher. Attending to print, staying on task by placing a finger under each word, turning the page, and locating the first word on each page is tedious for the at-risk reader. With persistence and determination, the teacher lovingly supports, redirects, and cues the students so they can complete this task successfully. The teacher might even have to hold the finger of some students and guide their pointing. She might need to alert the students to turn the page and find the first word with their finger. Many times the teacher turns the page for the students and points to the first word. Before proceeding, she waits until all students in the group have positioned a finger under the next word.

The first complete reading of the story is done without the students saying the words as the teacher reads them and is uninterrupted with discussion and comments. The repetitive reading portion of the Read Together activity is the proper time for conversation about the book.

Immediately following the first reading, the teacher directs the students to locate the cover of the book and place a finger under the title of the story. The teacher then invites the students to read the story aloud with her. Again, the teacher's task is to make sure the students are placing a finger under each word as they read. The book is read in unison at a rate slower than when reading alone, but at an adequate rate for the teacher to model good phrasing and expression. She does not read so slowly that the students must say the word first. In fact, the teacher should be reading a fraction of a second ahead of the students. She does not stop to study unknown words, but rather reads together with the students without interruption.

At the conclusion of the second reading, the students read aloud in unison, pointing to each word as they read. When the students hesitate in their reading, the teacher pronounces the word, prompts students to turn to the correct page, and makes sure each student is pointing and looking at the print.

Next the students work individually on the print by reading some portion of the book aloud. The teacher may direct the student to a specific page; she may ask them to read alternating pages front to back; or she may let the students select their favorite page to read. If the student has difficulty with a word, the teacher supplies the word. By this point, the students should be using their memory and their graphemic knowledge to decode the print. They should have a word-for-word match and correctly recall the word. Rather than a retelling of the story, this is a system in which the word that is read is the word in the text.

This concludes the first day of the Read Together activity. The process should progress from start to finish in one uninterrupted session. As intense as this activity is, it is essential in order to have the students gain control of the skills they must master to become good readers.

Procedure - Subsequent Days

For the remainder of the school week, the students should reread the Read Together book each day during the review portion of their Guided Reading Lesson. They may read the book as a group, the teacher may ask each student to read a portion of the book, or the teacher may allow the students to choose some portion to read to the group. In addition, the teacher may ask the students to read the book silently.

The teacher also may incorporate the review of the Read Together book in a number of practice activities. She may choose to have the students buddy-read the book, one student reading the book to the other. The students may take the book home as a homework assignment to read to their parents. The review reading may also be a practice activity during the time the students are at their desks. Having the students read the book into a tape recorder and then follow along as it is played back is an additionally helpful exercise.

The Read Together activity is an extremely beneficial learning activity. It combines the use of all the good reader strategies in a repetitive series of steps and is an instrumental element in the process of teaching reading to at-risk students.

Chapter Ten

Independent Reading Program

The independent reading level is the stage at which a student is able to read materials without help. Independent reading level material, written with a degree of difficulty, is read with ninety-five percent or above accuracy. The student has progressed to the independent reading level stage when he can read the material with fluency and virtual perfection.

The instructional reading level presents materials which a student is unable to read with comprehension and understanding without the teacher's instruction and support. When a student is reading at the instructional level, he is reading material with ninety percent accuracy. In other words, he is missing no more than one word in ten. Instructional level material means just that: only after the teacher has told the student everything he needs to know is he able to read the material. Her instruction allows the student to decipher any unknown elements of print — the names of the characters, the setting, vocabulary words, and any action in the story.

When a student is unable to read material with comprehension and understanding even after the teacher's instruction, he is at his frustration level. Attempting to work on materials at the frustration level forces the student to practice incorrect, ineffective strategies and guarantees reading failure.

Occasionally it is necessary for students to gather information from print which is at their frustration level, material read with less than ninety percent accuracy. In these instances, the teacher should tape record the material as she reads it to the students. They can then listen repeatedly to the tapes until they gain knowledge of the content of the material. It is possible for a student's listening comprehension level to allow him to understand and comprehend materials which are at his frustration level in reading. Materials that are read to students should be about two years above grade placement.

If there is one universal belief among educators about reading, it is that the reading abilities of students increase only when and if they practice reading. The positive effect on a student's reading abilities is immeasurable when they attend schools where they are allowed and encouraged to practice reading and when they live in homes in which the parents read to them. A student begins to choose to read on his own when he is in an environment where he is allowed to practice reading.

Imagine a swimming instructor who teaches by talking about and demonstrating various strokes to his students as they sit on the side of the pool. No amount of demonstration, videos, guest speakers, art projects or songs about swimming will teach his young students how to swim. The only way to learn how to swim is to get into the pool and practice.

In order for students to get good at something, they have to practice the whole act. In reading, this means practicing the reading of a book at the independent level. Arriving at this level requires hard, specific teaching on the part of the teacher and constant, regular practice on the part of the student.

There are a number of benefits to be gained from having a student read large amounts of easy material; that is, material written at the independent level. First, such material helps develop fluency. When at-risk readers are in the initial stages of reading, they cannot read a book the first time with fluency. It is only after they are taught the book, have received the teacher's help, support and encouragement while they read, and have read it several times under the teacher's supervision that they are able to read the book with fluency. Reading with fluency allows the student to begin reading in the voice of the author, reading with expression and reading using the grammatical markings.

Second, reading easy material develops efficient eye movement. Being able to read quickly across a line of print increases the ability to focus and develops proficient eye movement and return sweep. A student possesses few skills in the initial stages of learning to read, and his reading is constantly interrupted as he stops to think and work at deciphering the print. His eye movement, therefore, is also interrupted. This is a typical reading pattern characteristic of the instructional reading level, so by the time the student progresses to the independent reading level, he benefits from effective eye movement and return sweep.

Third, reading numerous books familiarizes students with language the way it appears in print which is enormously different from oral language. Students who have not been read to and those with auditory interference need intense work in developing their aptitude for the rules of written language. Reading a large number and variety of books teaches them to predict and guess and anticipate when they are reading unseen print. After students have been taught word recognition skills, the most natural and effective way to expose them to these words repeatedly is through the recreational reading of easy material.

Fourth, continued exposure to a large variety of books helps at-risk readers distinguish each word's visual characteristics. Reading in context builds a meaning vocabulary and increases the student's knowledge base. The benefits of an independent reading program and the practice of reading independently are vitally important. Because reading is such hard work for at-risk students, they never choose to read on their own. At-risk readers need help and encouragement, support and praise from the teacher in order to stay at the task of reading.

Antonio is a typical case in point. A Fifth grade student who read on the first grade level, Antonio had the added at-risk factor of having been retained. Antonio's teacher was able to move Antonio from reading on a first grade level to reading on a fourth grade level in about six months. As she talked with him about his reading progress, she asked him if he knew his reading was improving and that it was becoming easier. Antonio replied, "I know I can read better now, and I even like reading when you teach me my reading lessons." Then upon reflection he said, "But I still don't read on the bus and at home like some of those other kids."

In Antonio's mind, he could not imagine reading would ever be something he would want to pick up and do on his own. Developing a love for reading begins at an early age before students experience failure and involves a reading program that makes reading easy.

The independent reading program is an important part of an at-risk reader's instruction. Under the careful, watchful guidance of the teacher, at-risk readers spend as much time practicing the act of reading using real books as they spend being taught reading by their teacher. The goal in Early Detection Necessary Action is to have students practice reading books at the independent level at least forty-five minutes each day in addition to the Guided Reading Lesson, the Read Together and the Cut-up Story.

In the early stages of reading, the student's knowledge is meager.

In fact, the only books he is able to read are those the teacher has taught during the Guided Reading Lesson, the Read Together or the Cut-up Story. During the independent reading time, it is extremely important for the student to read books that are easy for him.

A structured independent reading program involves homework, silent reading, buddy reading, and a variety of reading activities from which the teacher may choose. For homework the student reads two books to his parents every night. These books, selected by the teacher, have been taught to him in previous weeks. She knows the student can read these book with at least ninety-five to 100 percent accuracy. The teacher places the books in a gallon, plastic zipper-type bag on which she has written the student's name and bus number and the teacher's name. On colored construction paper, the teacher duplicates the chart, "When you don't know a word, don't let it bug you" which she places in front of the bag. The chart helps the parent understand how to coach the student when he comes to an unknown word.

In the plastic bag is a checklist for the parent to initial indicating the student read the book. If the parent has not initialed the checklist, the student reads the books to the teacher, instructional aide or parent volunteer who tape records the reading. The student then listens to himself. The process, whether at home or at school, takes fifteen minutes of the student's forty-five minutes of independent reading time. The teacher monitors the collection of books, adding the new ones she has taught and removing the ones that have been in the collection for a longer period of time and that the student has read repeatedly.

A portion of the day is designated for silent reading. Previously taught books at the student's independent level are kept in a box, basket, or plastic tub. It is important for the student to be aware of the location of the books so that he has ready access to them. During silent reading time, a time designated and monitored by the teacher, the student selects from his known books enough titles to keep him engaged in reading for at least ten minutes. After the student has selected his books, he reads them silently.

It is often difficult to keep the at-risk student involved in reading during the sustained silent reading time. The teacher frequently must help him select books, insist that he stay on task, and support him while he is reading. The teacher might say, "Oh, I read that book and I really like it. I think you're going to like this part." Or "Read to the end and find out what happens and tell me."

If the teacher suspects the student has chosen a book that is too difficult for him to read, she might say to him, "Read some of that book into my ear," and after the student has read quietly to the teacher, she might say, "That book is too difficult for you. Reading is supposed to be easy. You don't need to try to make reading so difficult. Reading is always supposed to be easy." She selects a book, hands it to him and says, "I bet you'll find this book is easy." She helps him get started in the newly selected book, and after reading a page or two, the student is engaged in the act of reading.

After reading silently, the student shares reading time with a buddy, each student reading the titles of his choice. One student reads ten minutes to his buddy, and then the buddy reads ten minutes to him. This takes a total of twenty minutes with each student reading ten minutes.

At this point in the independent reading time, the student has read a total of thirty-five minutes: fifteen minutes reading homework books, ten minutes of silent reading, and ten minutes of buddy reading.

The additional ten minutes are flexible, but they are never optional. The teacher is free to choose from a variety of reading activities to complete the forty-five minutes of independent reading time. One method is oral impress where the teacher, parent volunteer, or instructional aide sits beside the student and they simultaneously read the book aloud. The adult sits so that the student is attentive to her, reads in an appropriate pace, and speaks in a low, soft voice so the student can easily follow along.

Another effective activity is choral reading with the whole group reading together a book, poem or play they have already been taught. The teacher sets the pace and intonation patterns so the reading does not deteriorate into a sing-song pattern. Attending to meaning as a way to determine intonation should be stressed.

A story party is another example. The teacher forms groups of four or five students who read at various levels. Each student chooses a story to read to his small group. Ample time for practicing the story is provided, particularly for the at-risk student who is supervised to make sure this is accomplished. The only student holding a book during the story party is the student who is reading. The others listen attentively. A story party has the benefit of engaging the student in meaningful oral reading as well as relieving the pressure of others identifying his errors, though students may ask him to repeat a part they did not understand or that did not make sense.

Having the at-risk student read to younger students is a wonderful way for him to receive needed practice reading independent level material without a loss of prestige. By becoming the teacher's helper, the older, disabled student goes to a kindergarten classroom to read aloud to a small group of students. The reader is required to practice reading the books before going to the classroom to assure reading success both for himself and for the younger students.

Another example is a group play. The Early Detection Necessary Action group selects or is assigned a character in a play previously taught during a Guided Reading Lesson. The students choose their character parts and read them. The students might perform the play for the classroom, though this is not necessary. It is enough that the reading of the play has given them an opportunity to read at their independent level and to practice doing the work of reading.

The goal of the independent reading program is to increase the reading ability of the at-risk student. The only way to accelerate a student in his reading ability is to give him time to practice the skills he must have in order to be a good reader. The more opportunities a teacher has to guide the at-risk student through a new book, then give him time to practice the book until it is at his independent level, the more rapid progress the at-risk student will make. It is a process that takes time, never less than forty-five minutes each day. More would be even better.

The time of the day set aside to have students practice independent reading does not include time spent looking at a book or swapping books or going to the library to check out a book. There is nothing wrong with any of these activities. In fact, there is nothing wrong with students looking at books and illustrations which are far above their independent reading level. A student's exploration of books that are far too difficult for him to read but which interest him is beneficial. But the time of the day set aside to have students practice independent reading means one thing: they must engage in the act of reading, and they must practice until they read with fluency and virtual perfection.

The management of an independent reading program involves a teacher's commitment to the ongoing organization of materials, dedication to the task of keeping the at-risk reader attentive to his responsibilities, and the ever-present knowledge that the at-risk student should never be made to feel different or set apart from the other students. An educator who embodied the spirit of a dedicated teacher committed to the success of her students is Mrs. Deborah Strickland. Mrs. Strickland, a career educator in Georgia, worked forty-five years as a reading teacher, a reading specialist, a reading supervisor, and a principal.

When she retired from her position as principal, Mrs. Strickland requested a teaching assignment, and for the last ten years of her career, she taught a second grade class. Her vision was to give her students the absolute best possible foundation in reading and in math, and, indeed, they moved forward faster with greater success than any others.

A large part of her success in the classroom resulted from her skill in managing the reading program and in particular, making sure her at-risk students were never singled out. She maintained three shelves of books in her classroom. One week she placed the books for the at-risk readers on the top shelf, the most difficult books on the bottom shelf and the average books on the middle shelf. After teaching a lesson to each group of students, she asked the at-risk students to choose books from the top shelf for their independent reading time; the more advanced readers to choose from the bottom shelf; and the average students, from the middle shelf.

After several weeks, Mrs. Strickland removed some books, added other titles, and changed the position of the shelves so that the students who were reading at a higher level now began taking books from the top shelf, the shelf where previously the at-risk readers selected their books; the at-risk readers chose books from the middle shelf; and the average readers, from the lower shelf.

Mrs. Strickland was a teacher who made it easy and simple for her students to select books at their independent level without a stigma attached. She realized the importance of not pointing out deficiencies or of having students feel singled out because of their reading abilities. Mrs. Strickland was a caring, supporting, loving teacher and one who knew that careful management and organization as well as constant supervision made reading a success for her students.

It is exceedingly important for teachers and educators to take charge of the independent reading program and to ensure their students are getting practice reading real books at their independent level.

Chapter Eleven

Selecting Appropriate Reading Materials

Learning to read is a sequential process. For the at-risk student to be successful, teachers must have appropriate material in sufficient quantities to teach the elements of print at each level. The books used in Early Detection Necessary Action are selected with several criteria in mind. At-risk readers need to have books with sufficient amounts of titles at each level. Each level needs to have a slight gradient of difficulty so the student is supported at one level as he is moving into the next, more difficult level. The books must have the correct elements of print. Equally important, the books must be readily available on a daily basis from the first day of school to the last.

It is unreasonable to expect an already overworked teacher to be responsible for finding appropriate books for her at-risk students. Because large quantities of books are needed each day, it is likewise not feasible for school libraries to supply them. Early Detection Necessary Action is a program that uses books which meet stringent criteria and which guarantees the teacher sufficient quantities of titles at each level to successfully teach her at-risk students.

The relationship between intelligence and beginning reading success varies from one reading program to another. A. I. Gates concluded that setting a "minimal age criteria" for learning to read is meaningless unless the materials, methods, and procedures used in the beginning reading program are analyzed. Additionally, the teacher's ability to adopt instruction to meet individual student's needs must be taken into account. G. D. Spache and E. B. Spache, authors of *Reading in the Elementary School,* believe it is the "stereotypical, inflexible, and mass-oriented reading program that demands a higher mental age and makes intelligence so important a factor in reading success in our primary schools."

Basal reading programs are complete packages of reading material and account for seventy to ninety percent of what goes on during reading periods in elementary classrooms. They are organized by grade level with students mastering print at one level before moving to the next. These reading series work for seventy percent of the students. They have never been the answer for students with at-risk factors. The books and materials used in basal reading programs are the only materials available for teachers to use with students. The teacher follows all the instructions in the teacher manual, uses all the prescribed activities, and if the student does not advance in his knowledge of print at that level, she has two options.

In the first option, the teacher proceeds with the student using the same materials and supplying the same instruction she provides for the students who have mastered print at this level. The teacher reads the stories to the students, tape records the stories and has the students listen. The teacher asks a more advanced student to read to a student who is unable to read for himself. Evaluation of the student's progress is accomplished through a reading "test" which the teacher reads to the student, and the student answers orally. The problem is that reading a reading test for the student does not evaluate the student's reading abilities. Reading a reading test for the student only evaluates the student's listening comprehension.

This practice may build a background of experience for the story, increase the student's receptive vocabulary and help the student become familiar with the structure of language in print, but it does nothing to help the student gain the skills necessary to become a reader. Only when the student is doing the work of reading does he become a reader. Reading differs from listening and talking in that reading requires the ability to match sounds and symbols, follow a line of print, interpret, and understand how the actual print converts to words and thoughts.

Educators may rationalize that students who are not making progress at least do not suffer a lack of esteem because their books are the same books being taught to their peers. In actuality, the opposite is true. Rather than building self-esteem as a reader, the student is constantly reminded that he cannot read and that someone else must read for him. The at-risk student is demoralized by this practice. He becomes depressed and angry at the idea that he must rely on someone to read for him. And when educators do not acknowledge his reading problem, the student is filled with panic and desperation, for he realizes he cannot read and thinks he is the only one who knows. In his mind, how can he possibly seek help from a teacher who does not acknowledge his problem?

The teacher's second option is to take the student back through the same material if, upon completing the first primer or readiness section of the reading program, a student has not mastered and cannot move into the next level of print. This time she teaches the book more slowly, often talking louder and more deliberately to the student as she is teaching. Such has been the practice for many years, and time and time again it has been proved unsuccessful. Students who are taken back through the same books and activities that did not work the first time are guaranteed no greater success the next time.

Basal readers control the sight words and meaning words. Students work with a few words, reading a book where the sight words are used over and over.

Go, go, go.
Go.
Go in.
I will go.
I will go in.
I will not go.
I will not go in.

The problem with this type of print is that no story is created. In addition, using these types of materials and teaching methods, it is not unreasonable for a group of at-risk first grade students to be in school for six months and have read and worked with a total of only five words.

Many students do not understand print in the conventional manner. At-risk students develop many ineffective, incorrect coping strategies to deal with print. They may remember that the word *will* has four marks or two tall sticks. Many just guess. They know the word is one of five and they begin to call the words, *go, I, will*. By the expression on the teacher's face, the student knows when he has guessed the correct word, and he proceeds to the next word and begins the guessing process again.

Other students listen for someone to tell them the word. Students rely on the wrong strategies to unlock print. They are not using the correct strategies that transfer to the next level of unfamiliar print.

The students who have no at-risk factors quickly move through the pre-primer books and begin reading books with increasingly higher levels of print. The teacher has many books in her room for these students. They read literature books from the library, and with their rapid progress in reading, they are able to read their text books, as well. They get more and more reading practice and continue to move forward in their reading abilities.

The teacher does not have books in her room to provide appropriate instruction and practice for the at-risk student. The at-risk student cannot go to the library and find books written at his level of print, nor is he capable of reading his textbooks. So, by the design of the basal reading program and materials, the student who needs more instruction and practice at each level does not receive it.

The Remedial Basal Series designed to be used with at-risk readers has some major flaws. When a program is heavy in phonics, encourages the use of phonics tapes and videos—as many of the programs on the market do—and teaches students to use one minor segment of their word recognition skills, students begin to rely on those techniques and believe what they have learned is reading. Programs that teach students only one way to decode print do not combine and interrelate all of the word recognition skills necessary to become a good reader. The student becomes more disabled, and it becomes more difficult for the teacher to move him forward.

The Language Experience approach uses a student's own language as the basis of reading instruction. It brings all aspects of the communication process together in a unified curriculum. The teacher records groups of stories on language experience charts. These stories are then used as instructional reading material from which the teacher begins teaching words, phrases, selected word recognition skills, and some comprehension skills. Later the teacher places students in smaller groups and continues the development of experience stories.

In order for the language experience approach to be successful, the teacher must be a skilled, knowledgeable, and experienced reading teacher, and even at that, the most skilled, dedicated teacher does not have time to develop the books and materials to accelerate the at-risk reader.

Computer programs where students sit and work on word skill activities may make the student better at those skills in isolation, but students do not have books to read and therefore cannot practice the whole act of reading.

To understand the importance of having books with the correct gradient of difficulty, it is necessary to understand the reading tasks of beginning readers. To read two words or more in a series, the student must, in essence, over learn and be able to immediately pronounce structure words like *the* or *a*. All nouns, other than the names of people or places, are preceded by either *the* or *a*. At this stage in a reading program, caption books that control the sight words but not the meaning words are used. Various techniques of teaching caption books ensure a student has over learned the lesson.

For example, a book entitled, *Toys*, presents extremely supportive illustrations of each toy on the page. The student reads, *The ball. The bat. The skate. The puzzle.* He looks at the picture cues and illustrations that provide the meaning cues and decides which word makes sense based on the beginning of the meaning word. The teacher teaches the students the sight word *the*. Using a visualizing approach, she talks about the *th* words.

A book entitled *Babies* supplies text and supporting picture cues: *He eats. He cries. He laughs. He sleeps.* The teacher teaches the word *he* and other words that fall into the same, general pattern: *we*, *me* and *the*. She teaches the letter *h,* explaining it is the sound at the beginning of *horse*, *house*, *he*, and *home*. She shows the difference between a capital *H* and a lower case *h*.

The teacher introduces sight words, and she helps the students practice the beginning consonant and meaning in order to decode meaning words. Illustrations in caption books aid the student in using meaning to decode. The student is taught books at the caption level until he has mastered the sight words and the beginning consonants he needs for that level.

Students are taught the consonant/vowel/consonant pattern words as sets of phonemic spelling patterns at the caption book level. The student now reads, *The man. The fan. The pan.* or *The boy. The toy*. Because it is impossible to put such words into a natural language context without some form of action, verbs are supplied.

Now the students move into phrase books. *The man ran. The boy ran. The girl ran.* The teacher presents the consonant/vowel/consonant pattern word *an*. The student is once again over learning the sight word *the* and is using initial consonants and meaning to decode the meaning words.

Another example: *I like apples. I like ice cream. I like cake*. The sight word is *I*. The consonant/vowel/consonant plus *e* phonemic spelling pattern using the word *like* is taught and practiced, and the student uses beginning sounds and picture cues to decode the meaning words.

The next level of print adds variant endings: *I like running. I like reading. I like singing.* The student reviews the sight word *like*, reviews the *ike* phonemic spelling pattern, and is taught the *ing* ending.

More complex sentences follow: *The man ran after the dog. The dog ran after the cat.* The new element of print is the word *after.* Subsequent books introduce grammatical features, such as quotation marks, and dialogue words, such as the word *said* as in these examples: *"I like to run," said dad. "I like to swim," said mom. "I like to climb," said baby.*

By the end of the first grade reading level, reading materials include a series of consecutive sentences on each page. With sufficient pre-reading, vocabulary words and word analysis skills followed by silent reading, oral reading, and independent reading, many new words become over learned and immediately pronounceable.

Beginning at-risk readers need to be taught from real books which control the sight words and the elements of print, but not the meaning words. The books should have a gradient of difficulty. As the student masters the sight words and elements of print at one level, he then moves to the next level. The illustrations should support the text and help the student use meaning to decode new vocabulary words. In order to teach at-risk students to become good readers and accelerate them in their reading abilities, teachers must have appropriate books at each level in sufficient quantities.

Traditionally at-risk readers are repeatedly taught the same book. Many programs designed for at-risk readers do not have books for the students to practice the whole act of reading. Consequently, students who need more practice on each level receive less. They complete phonic worksheets, sit at a computer screen doing word analysis skills, listen to tapes of phonetic sounds, or watch videos and make sounds with the moderator. If a reading program does not use real books, do not consider it appropriate for any student, especially not for at-risk students.

After several years of implementing the Early Detection Necessary Action program in an elementary school, the curriculum director saw the need to establish and develop a similar, appropriate reading program for disabled students in the middle school. In her search, she called major textbook publishers and asked them to preview their programs with her. One company representative presented her with a reading program based on audio cassettes and phonetic worksheets. After the presentation, the curriculum director asked, "Where are the books?" The sales representative replied, "Oh, we don't use books with this program." Having witnessed firsthand the success of the Early Detection Necessary Action program, a program based on the use of real books, the curriculum director responded, "Well, we won't be adopting a reading program that doesn't have books." In order to learn to read, a student must practice reading using real books.

The books used in Early Detection Necessary Action are carefully chosen. While they are not written specifically to teach at-risk readers, they are excellent for this purpose. The level of print and the student's instructional level are matched. The books are short and generally have one story so the student can complete a book in one sitting. They provide enough practice at each level of print to enable the at-risk reader to acquire knowledge at a specific level before moving to the next. There is a slight gradient of difficulty at each level so the student gradually moves from one stage to the next. The books that are chosen control the sight words and the elements of print, but they do not control the meaning words. The illustrations are extremely supportive in giving the expectancy clues the student needs in order to use meaning to decode.

Most basal readers control both the sight words and the meaning words. Real literature books are written to get a burning message across or to entertain or influence an opinion. In literature books, nothing is controlled, not sight words, meaning words, structure of language in print, illustrations, or the concept being presented. The author's aim is to have the reader experience the content of the book through print. Students need to be exposed to literature books, and many literature books can be used with at-risk readers. But literature books are extremely expensive, particularly when numerous copies of the same title are required for the proper teaching of at-risk students. Expecting teachers to use only real literature books for emergent, at-risk readers limits the number of appropriate books available for this purpose.

Appropriate books for at-risk students are those which are written at the student's instructional level where the teacher can teach him what he needs to know to read the book and where the student can practice what he has been taught. The teacher must be supplied with enough books so this can be repeated day after day.

In her book, *Reading: The Patterning of Complex Behavior,* Marie

Clay describes a study where observation records tallied the number of words read. The observation records represent one-sixth of the student's reading experience per week. Using this estimate, Clay found that the student who made superior progress read something in excess of twenty thousand words in his first year of instruction, the high-progress middle student read fifteen thousand words, the lower middle student read ten thousand words and the low student read less than five thousand words.

The study points out how the materials used and the instructional organization makes accelerating the at-risk reader difficult. When the student who makes rapid progress is taught his reading lesson, the lesson takes longer and he reads more words. If the at-risk student reads the entire book used in his instructional lesson, he only reads at best thirty words. The high-progress student reads five hundred words in his lesson.

If at-risk readers are taught, and then read ten books with fifty words at the same time as the rapid progress student is taught one book with five hundred words, then the at-risk reader has been given the same opportunity to make progress. Reading programs are not and have never been designed to give at-risk readers equal reading mileage.

Clearly it does not make sense to take students who need more practice and place them in a program where they get less practice. In Early Detection Necessary Action, one of the goals is to teach the student, then have him practice and read as many words each day as the high-progress student.

Epilogue

All students can be fluent readers if they are taught to read using methods that address their special learning needs. The key is to identify students who are at risk of developing reading disabilities and teach them to read while they are young.

The material contained in this book identifies the at-risk factors which characterize students for whom reading will be difficult and cites diagnostic tools for measuring the extent of those at-risk characteristics in each child. Also, as you review the strategies good readers use when they come to a word they do not know, you will recognize that at-risk readers lack necessary strategies to aid them in decoding print.

In other words, you will understand what *Early Detection* is all about. Armed with this knowledge, the next step is *Necessary Action*, that part of the E.D.N.A. program which gives you the skills to teach at-risk children how to read, to accelerate them in their reading, and, ultimately, to make them independent readers.

To be effective, a reading program must utilize a variety of techniques. It must give the student the opportunity to practice reading real books at the student's instructional level; that is, when the student can read with ninety percent accuracy, missing no more than ten percent of the words. It must guarantee constant monitoring which tells the teacher what a student knows, what he does not know, and what needs to be done next. It identifies the student's strengths and weaknesses.

An effective reading program provides the tools to measure a student's progress. It focuses on individual learning and enables the student to employ a self-improvement system to aid him when he comes to a word he does not know. An effective reading program prevents the student from practicing his disability. It permits oral reading which improves a student's oral language and enables the teacher to make instructional decisions regarding what to teach. It encourages persistence in silent reading. It improves a student's concept of print. It allows for a small group setting around a table where the teacher is able to keep the students at the task of reading. It constantly rewards and encourages.

An effective reading program provides learning activities which are based on the principle that the teacher must tell the student everything he needs to know in order to be a successful reader. It permits the teacher to talk the students through the pictures before reading the story, and it engages the students in conversation. An effective reading program builds a meaning vocabulary and provides purposes for print. It gives the student numerous occasions to read easy material as well as material which is at his instructional level. Most importantly, an effective reading program provides an opportunity for the student to practice the skills used by fluent readers.

Teaching reading is much like coaching an athlete. A good coach determines the athlete's ability and then develops a program at that ability level. The program incorporates all the skills the athlete needs to perform well. If the athlete is practicing a skill using ineffective strategies, the coach explains how the athlete needs to change, then gives him time and instruction to practice it correctly, using the proper form. With the support, encouragement, and help of the coach, the athlete works to constantly improve.

Good reading coaches follow the same practices. Just as a coach determines the athlete's ability and develops a program that is at the athlete's ability level, so, too, must a reading teacher proceed with her students. A good reading teacher determines the student's reading level and implements an effective learning program which integrates all the skills the student needs to perform well.

Teaching a student to read using books that are at his independent reading level eliminates the possibility of his struggling with print that is too difficult. Material that is above his independent level forces the student to use ineffective reading strategies which can cause him to regress in his reading abilities. A student can develop disabling practices in as short a time as six weeks. The student has to have an opportunity to practice fluent reader strategies. Reading should always be easy enough so that the student can practice perfect reading form. Practice makes permanent. Correct practice makes perfect.

In order to make a good, fluent reader out of a student who has been identified as having at-risk characteristics, a learning plan must be implemented which is designed specifically for him and which is founded on the principles of an effective reading program. In addition to teaching him how to read, it gives him constant practice doing what good readers do.

Failure Is Not An Option flows out of ongoing staff development programs — Early Detection Necessary Action (E.D.N.A.) — which train classroom teachers to identify, diagnose and accelerate non-readers early in their school years by addressing the needs of those at-risk students in their regular classrooms. E.D.N.A. is an early intervention program designed to be implemented in kindergarten and in first, second, and third grades.

For Those Who Want More Help

E.D.N.A. is a supplemental instructional reading program individually tailored to fit into the existing structure and organization of the school. Therefore, other students in the classroom who are reading at their grade level will continue to use the current reading program. E.D.N.A. works within the resources and organizational framework in each school system to build on what is available and to make it as effective for at-risk readers as possible. The program may be implemented one grade level at a time, used only by Title I teachers, or it may be completely implemented at once by all kindergarten through third grade teachers.

Failure Is Not An Option and the Early Detection Necessary Action program prepare teachers to teach students who do not learn to read using the traditional approach. The program is organized so that teachers have appropriate books and materials in sufficient quantities to teach at-risk readers every day. A plan is developed to monitor students' progress and to make adjustments in instruction. Additionally, the organization of the program is such that teachers receive constant support as they teach the at-risk readers in their classrooms.

The training program contains the five essential elements found in effective staff development programs: presentation, modeling, practice, feedback, and coaching. The initial five-day training course takes place in a traditional classroom setting, and may be scheduled on successive days or spread out over a period of time. Kindergarten, first and second grade teachers may all be trained during the same five sessions.

After the initial training, teachers begin using the program with their students. A lesson is modeled during an on-site visit early in the implementation period. Teachers then meet in a follow-up session for a review of the program and to have questions, problems and concerns addressed.

After training and modeling, additional follow-up days focus on supporting teachers as they put effective practices for at-risk readers to work. Additionally, three follow-up days per grade level are scheduled over a period of time. Teachers are provided lesson plans, books, and teaching materials to teach at-risk readers from the first day of school to the last.

At least one person in leadership at the school level needs to participate in the training. The administration in the school is advised to set up a system to provide the vital monitoring and feedback to make the program work. Similarly, a contact person at the school level is assigned to communicate with the E.D.N.A. trainer and to supervise the distribution and rotation of the E.D.N.A. books and materials within the school. Of utmost importance is the dedication by administrators and teachers alike to teach the E.D.N.A. group daily.

Above all, the administration as well as the teachers must keep attention focused on reading and possess the determination to keep expectations high.

When E.D.N.A. is in place, the results are astounding:
- Once a teacher has been trained, she will be able to teach any student to read.
- Every first grade student will be reading by December.
- All students will read to their potential by the end of third grade.

Bibliography

Aaron, Ira E. *Word Recognition Skills Instruction.* Atlanta, GA: Georgia Department of Education, 1982.

Aaron, Robert L. "Helping Remedial Readers Master the Reading Vocabulary Through a Seven Step Method." Unpublished manuscript, 1979.

Adams, M.J. *Beginning to Read: Thinking and Learning About Print.* Cambridge: MIT Press, 1983.

Allington, R.L. 1977. "If They Don't Read Much, How They Ever Gonna Get Good?"
Journal of Reading, 21: 57-61.
1980. "Poor Readers Don't Get to Read Much in Reading Groups." *Language Arts,* 57: 872-877.
1991. "The Legacy of Slow It Down and Make It More Concrete." J. Zutel and S. McCormick (eds.), *Learner Factors/Teacher Factors: Issues in Literacy Research and Instruction,* 19-30. Chicago: National Reading Conference.
1994. "What's Special About Special Programs for Children Who Find Learning to Read Difficult?" *Journal of Reading Behaviors,* 26: 1-21.
and McGill, Franzen, A.1989. "School Response to Reading Failure: Chapter I and Special Education Students in Grades 2, 4, & 8." *Elementary School Journal,* 89: 529-542.

Anderson, R.C. and Freebody, P. 1981. "Vocabulary Knowledge." J.T. Guthrie (ed.) *Comparison and Teaching: Research Perspectives.* Newark, DE: International Reading Association. E. J. Hiebert, J.A. Scott, and I.G.. Wilkinson. "Becoming a Nation of Readers." Champaign. IL; University of Illinois,

Center for the Study of Reading. 1983.
E.H. Hiebert, J.A. Scott, and I.G. Wilkinson. "Becoming a Nation of Readers: The Report of the Commission on Reading." Washington, DC: National Institute of Education, 1985.

Applebee, Arthur N. March, 1981. "Looking at Writing " *Education Leadership*, 38.

Archer, M.P. 1960. "Building a Vocabulary With a Fourth Grade Class." *Elementary English*, 37: 447-448.

Artley, A.S. 1943. "Teaching Word Meanings through Context." *Elementary English Review*, 20: 68-74.
1975. "Words, Words, Words." *Language Arts*, 52: 1067-1072.

Bailey, M.H. 1967. "The Utility of Phonics Generalizations in Grades One Through Six." *The Reading Teacher*: 413-418.

Baumann, J.F. "The Effectiveness of a Direct Instruction Paradigm for Teaching Main Idea Comprehension." *Reading Research Quarterly*, 20: 93-115.

"Becoming a Nation of Readers: The Report of the Commission on Reading" Washington, DC: National Institute of Education. 1985.

Benton, A.L. *Right-Left Discrimination and Finger Localization*. New York: Paul B. Hoeber, 1959.

Blachowitz, C. 1986. "Making Connections: Alternatives to the Vocabulary Notebook."
Journal of Reading, 29: 643-649.

Brophy, J. 1988. "Research Linking Teacher Behaviors to Student Achievements: Potential Implications for Instruction of Chapter I Students." *Educational Psychologist*, 123: 235-286.

Bryant, P.E., L. Bradley, M. Maclean, and I. Crossland. 1989. "Nursery Rhymes, Phonological Skills and Reading." *Journal of Child Language*, 16: 407-428.

Carbo, Marie. *How to Record Books for Maximum Reading Gains.* New York: National Reading Styles Institute, Inc., 1979.

Chall, J. *Learning to Read: The Great Debate.* New York: McGraw Hill, 1967.

Children's Defense Fund. *The State of America's Children.*

Clay, Marie. *The Early Detection of Reading Difficulties.* New Zealand: Heinemann Education, 1979.
The Early Detection of Reading Difficulties: A Diagnostic Survey with Recovery Procedures (3rd. Ed). Exeter, NH: Heinemann. 1985.
The Early Detection of Reading Difficulties. Auckland, New Zealand: Heinemann. 1985.
Reading: The Patterning of Complex Behavior. (2nd Ed.) Auckland, New Zealand: Heinemann Educational Book. 1976.
What Did I Write? Beginning Writing Behavior. New Zealand: Heinemann Educational Books, 1975.
"Observing Young Readers, " selected papers. 66-87. Heinemann Educational Books. Portsmouth, NH
M. Gill, T. McNaughton, and K. Salmon. *Record of Oral Language and Blks and Gutches.* New Zealand: Heinemann Publishers, 1983.

Clymer, T. "The Utility of Phonic Generalization In the Primary Grades." *The Reading Teacher*, 252-258.

Cook, David L. , O.D. When *Your Child Struggles, The Myths of 20/20 Vision What Every Parent Needs to Know.* Atlanta, GA : Invision Press, 1992.

Cramer, R.L. 1975. "Reading to Children: Why and How." *The Reading Teacher*, 28: 460-463.

Cunningham, P.M. 1975-76. "Investigating a Synthesized Theory of Mediated Word Identification." *Reading Research Quarterly*, 11: 127-143.
1980. "Applying a Compare/Contrast Process to Identifying Polysyllabic Words." *Journal of Reading Behavior.*

Phonics They Use. Harper Collins College Publishers, 1995.
and J. Cunningham. 1992. "Making Words: Enhancing the Invented Spelling-Decoding Connection." *The Reading Teacher*, Vol. 46, No. 2.

DeHirssch, Katrina, J. Jansky, and W.J. Longford. *Predicting The Failing Reader.*
Harper and Row, New York, 1966.

Dolch, E. *Dolch Basic Sight Vocabulary*. Champaign, Ill.: Garrard Publishing, 1953.

Durkin, D. *Teaching Them to Read*. Boston, Allyn and Bacon, 1978. *Teaching Young Children to Read*. (3rd. Ed.) Boston: Allyn & Bacon

Fallan, M., B. Bennett, and C. Rolheiser-Bennett. 1990. "Linking Classroom and School Improvement Educational Leadership." 47: 13-19.

Flax, N. May, 1970. "Problems in Relating Visual Functions to Reading Disorder." *American Journal Optometry and Archives American Academy of Optometry*: 366-372.
R. Mozlin, H.A. Solan. June 1984. "Learning Disabilities, Dyslexia, and Vision." *Journal American Optometric Association*: 399-403.

Forrester, A. Nov. 1977. "What Teachers Can Learn From Natural Readers." *The Reading Teacher*, Vol. 31: 160-166.

Fry, E. *Elementary Reading Instruction*. New York: McGraw-Hill, 1977.
1980. "The New Instant Word List." *The Reading Teacher*, 34: 284-290.

Gates, A.I. 1937. "The Necessary Mental Age for Reading." *Elementary School Journal*, 497-508.

Gentry, J.R. and J.W. Gillet. *Teaching Kids to Spell*. Portsmouth, NH: Heinemann. 1993.

Glass, G.G. and E. H. Burton. 1973. "How Do They Decode? Verbalizations and Observed Behaviors of Successful Decoders." *Education*, 94: 58-65.

Glazer, Susan M., Lyndon W. Searfoss, Lance M. Gentile. *Reexamining Reading Diagnosis*. Newark, Delaware: International Reading Association, 1995.

Goodman, K. *What's Whole in Whole Language?* Portsmouth, NH: Heinemann, 1986.
1969. "Analysis of Oral Reading Miscues: Applied Psycholinguistics."
Reading Research Quarterly, 5.
"Do you have to be Smart to Read? Do You Have to Read to be Smart?"
The Reading Teacher, 28: 625-632.
S. Readings: A Psycholinguistic Guessing Game. In Senger, H and Ruddell, R.B. (Eds.) Theoretical Models and Processes of Reading. "Theoretical Models and Processes of Reading" Newark: International Reading Association, 1970. C. Black.
"Dialect Barriers to Reading Comprehension: Revisited."
The Reading Teacher, October 1973.
C. Buck. "Dialect Barriers to Reading Comprehension Revisited."
The Reading Teacher, 22: 6-12.

Goodman, Y.M. 1978. "Kid-watching: An Alternative to Testing."
National Elementary Principal, 10: 41-45.
1981. "Review of Concepts About Print." *The Reading Teacher*, 34: 4.
and C.L. Burke. *Reading Miscue Inventory Manual: Procedure for Diagnosis and Remediation*. New York: MacMillan. 1972.

Graves, D. *Writing: Teachers and Children at Work*. Exter, NH: Heinemann.
Research Update: What Children Show us About Revision.
Language Arts, 56. 312-319.

Gunning, Thomas G. 1995. "Word Building: A Strategic Approach To the Teaching of Phonics." *The Reading Teacher,* Vol. 48, No. 6.

Guthrie, J.T. 1982. "Effective Teaching Practices." *The Reading Teacher*, 35: 766-768.

Hanson, I.W. 1966. "First Grade Children Work With Variant Endings." *The Reading Teacher*, 505-507.

Huberman, M. "School Improvement Strategies That Work: Some Scenarios."
Education Leadership, 41, 23-27.

Irwin, J.W. and C.A. Davis. 1980. "Assessing Readability: The Checklist Approach."
Journal of Reading, 24, 124-130.

Johnson, D.D. and P.D. Pearson. *Teaching Reading Vocabulary.* New York: Holt Reinhart and Winston, 1978.

Juel, C. 1990. "Effects of Reading Group Assignment on Reading Development in First and Second Grade." *Journal of Reading Behavior*, 22: 233-254.

Kavner, R. *Your Child's Vision: A Parent's Guide to Seeing, Growing, and Developing.* Simon & Shuster, Inc., New York, NY, 1985.

Kibby, M.W. "Passage Readability Affects the Oral Reading Strategies of Disabled Readers." *The Reading Teacher*, 32: 390-396.

Kirby, D. and T. Liner. *Inside Out: Developmental Strategies for Teaching Writing.* Montclair, NJ: Boynton/Cook. 1981.

Kozol, Jonathan. *Illiterate America.*

Marchbanks, G. and H. Levin. 1965. "Cues By Which Children Recognize Words."
Journal of Educational Psychology: 57-61.

Marzano, Robert J., Debra Pickering, Jay McTighe. *Assessing Student Outcomes Performance Assessment Using the Dimensions of Learning Model*. Alexandria VA: Association for Supervision and Curriculum Development, 1993.

Mason, J.M. "Early Reading from a Developmental Perspective," P.D. Pearson (Ed.) Handbook of Reading Research. New York: Longman.

McCormik, S. *Instructing Students Who Have Literacy Problems*. Columbus, Ohio: Merrill. 1995.

McFeely, D.C. 1974. "Syllabication Usefulness in a Basal and Social Studies Vocabulary."
The Reading Teacher: 809-814.

Moon, C. and C.D. Wells. "The Influences of Home on Learning to Read." *Journal of Research in Reading*, 16: 273-288.

Oillila, L., T. Johnson, and J. Downing, 1974. "Adapting Russian Methods of Auditory Discrimination Training for English" 1138-1141.

Paradis, E.E. 1974. "The Appropriateness of Visual Discrimination Exercises in Reading Readiness Material." *Journal of Educational Research*, 276-278.

Perfetti, C.A. and Hogaboam, T. 1975. "The Relationship Between Single Word Decoding and Reading Comprehension Skills." *Journal of Educational Psychology*, 67: 461-469.

Peters, H.B. 1961. "Screening With a Snellen Chart." *American Journal of Optometry and Archives of American Academy of Optometry*, 487-505.

Powell, D. and D. Hornsby, D., *Learning Phonics and Spelling in a Whole Language Classroom.* New York: Scholastics Professional Books, 1993.

Reid, J.F. 1966. "Learning to Think about Reading," Educational Research 9.

Samuels, S.J. 1988. "Decoding and Automaticity: Helping Poor Readers Become Automatic at Word Recognition." *The Reading Teacher*, 41: 756-760.
1973. "Success and Failure in Learning to Read: A Critique of the Research."
Reading Research Quarterly, 200-239.
and Alan E. Farstrup. " What Research Has to Say About Reading Instruction." Newark, Delaware: International Reading Association. 1992.

Santa, C.M. 1976-1977. "Spelling Patterns and the Development of Flexible Word Recognition Strategies." *Reading Research Quarterly*, 12: 125-144.

Schell, L.M. 1967. "Teaching Structural Analysis." *The Reading Teacher*: 133-137.

Shepard, L.A. and M.L. Smith. Flunking Grades: Research and Policies on Retention. Introduction and Overview: 1-15. Philadelphia: Falmen. 1989.
1990. "Synthesis of Research on Grade Retention." *Educational Leadership* 47: 84-88.

Slavin, R., N. Karweit, N. Madden *Effective Programs for Students at Risk.*
Boston: Allyn and Bacon, 1989.
N. Madden. 1989. "What Works for Students at Risk: A Research Synthesis" *Educational Leadership*, 46: 4-13.

Spache, G.D. and E. B. Spache. *Reading in the Elementary School.* Allyn and Bacon, 1977.

Stahl, S.A. 1992. "Saying the 'p' Word: Nine Guidelines for Exemplary Phonics Instruction." *The Reading Teacher*, 45: 618-625.
1986. Three Principles of Effective Vocabulary. *Journal of Reading* 29: 662-668.

Strickland, D. and others. 1977. "Reading and Pre-First Grade." *The Reading Teacher*, 780-781.

Suchoff, I.B. December 1981. "Research on the Relationship Between Reading and Vision — What Does It Mean?" *Journal of Learning Disabilities*, pages 573-576.

Tricman, R. 1985. "Onsets and Rimes as Units of Spoken Syllables: Evidence from Children." *Journal of Experimental Child Psychology*, 39: 161-181.

Tummer, W.E., and A.R. Nesdale. 1985. "Phonemic Segmentation Skill and Beginning Reading." *Journal of Educational Psychology*, 7: 417-427.

United Nations

United States Department of Education

Venezky, R.L., D.F. Kaestle, & A.M. Sun. "Literacy: A Profile of American Young Adults." Princeton, NJ: *Educational Testing Service National Assessment of Educational Progress.*

Vernon, M.D. 1962. "Specific Dyslexia." *British Journal of Educational Psychology, 143*-150.

Wardlaugh, R. 1966. "Syl•lab•i•ca•tion." *Elementary English*, 785-788.

Wood, K.D. and Robinson, N. 1983. "Vocabulary, Language, and Prediction: A Pre-reading Strategy." *The Reading Teacher,* 36: 4, 392-395

Wylie, R.E. and Durrell. 1970. "Teaching Vowels Through Phonograms." *Elementary English*, 787-791.